CRAZY *Healthy* with 4 ingredients

Dessert, Snack & Breakfast Recipes

Reviews

"It's such a fantastic and helpful concept.. Dee also includes an incredibly helpful capsule pantry guide" - Lexi Harrison and Beth Sinclair, crowdedkitchen.com

"Dee managed to combine simplicity, convenience and taste in such a beautiful way. I highly recommend it!" - Kim-Julie Hansen, founder of bestofvegan.com, and author of *Vegan Reset*

"If you like healthy, fuss-free recipes that don't require tons of ingredients, you need this book!" - Nisha Vora, rainbowplantlife.com, and author of *The Vegan Instant Pot Cookbook*

"A cookbook that starts with a chapter just dedicated to chocolate clearly GETS me. But what really caught my attention with this book is that every single recipe is made with just 4 ingredients (although from the creativity of these recipes you wouldn't guess it)" - Natalie Thomas, feastingonfruit.com

"If you are just trying to incorporate some more plants into your diet, Dee's recipes are sure to impress!" - Francesca Bonadonna, plantifullybased.com

"As a busy mom I appreciate that each recipe can be made quickly with minimal kitchen equipment and only 4 ingredients" - Corey Taylor, thevegansix.com

Dessert, Snack & Breakfast Recipes

Dee Dine
creator of Green Smoothie Gourmet
a plant-based recipe blog

LWP
Winston Little Publishing

Printed in USA
Winston Little Publishing
winstonlittlepublishing.com

Library of Congress Cataloging-in-Publication Data
2019916062
Dine, Dee
Crazy Healthy with 4 ingredients : Dessert, breakfast & snack vegan Recipes
Dee Dine, creator of Green Smoothie Gourmet
ISBN 9781732581807
1. Healthy Recipe Book 2. Healthy Dessert Book 3. Easy cooking- Recipes
Title: Crazy Healthy with 4 ingredients : Dessert, breakfast & snack vegan Recipes
Series: Crazy Healthy with 4 ingredients

Special orders are available via direct contact through publisher. Organizations, companies and individuals can arrange for a custom edition through the marketing director at the publisher's website.

Front cover design and interior photographs by Dee Dine

for my husband, three girls,
and all my inspiring followers on Instagram,
and my blog at Green Smoothie Gourmet

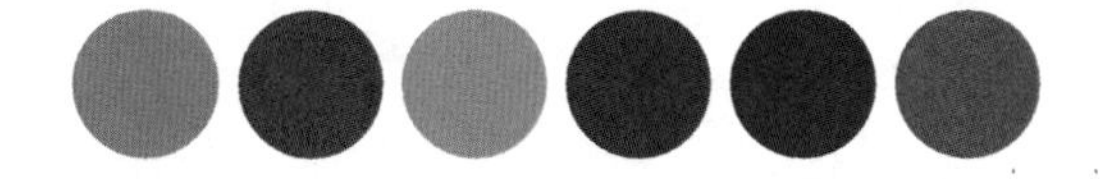

Table of Contents

Hello! Start Here

Welcome to the electronic version of the print book, "Crazy Healthy with 4 Ingredients," a healthy cookbook on sale as a beautiful color-coded paperback. This convenient electronic download is formated exactly the same, with color-coded nutritional targets, and is suitable for viewing on phones, tablets and computer.
This version provides another way to access most of easy 4-ingredient plant-based recipes that are powerfully nutritious and delicious. And offers an easy way to print out the Capsule Pantry list at the end.
Enjoy!

EASY, NUTRITIOUS, AFFORDABLE - RECIPES FOR EVERYONE

Conventional wisdom is pretty clear. One way to feel great is to eat more vegetables and less processed foods. Coincidently, my recipes use lots of vegetables and less processed foods. So think of my book as a stepping stone to healthier eating.
Whether you want to make a sweeping diet change or just want to add a few healthy plant-based recipes into your day, you'll find this book an easy route.
My recipes take advantage of a *capsule pantry* - a short list of healthy, whole food ingredients that can be mixed and matched to create multiple recipes.
The idea of a *capsule pantry* springs from the more familiar fashion concept of a *capsule wardrobe*, the practice of filling your closet with only a few essential items that can work together in multiple ways to produce many different outfits.
With a *capsule pantry* stocked based on my provided pantry list at the back of this book, you can not only make these recipes on a whim, but also create your own healthy minimal-ingredient foods.
Busy families, singles and college students who want to eat healthier with minimal

time, effort and investment will especially benefit from this book.

COMMON INGREDIENTS USED IN UNUSUAL WAYS

Not only are these recipes built with a simplified list of ingredients, the ingredients are often common, and easy to access. We are talking foods like spinach, cauliflower, avocado, quinoa, chocolate, berries, coconut, sweet potatoes, zucchini, nuts, seeds, lemons and the like. A few recipes use trendy superfoods, such as spirulina, matcha and baobab powder. In those recipes, sometimes I offer a more common ingredient swap or I provide an additional use so the purchase isn't one-off.

While many of the ingredients may be traditional, I often use them in unusual ways. As with the recipes on my blog, you'll find recipes with hidden veggies and other healthy foods in unexpected places.

Think lentil chocolate cups. Quinoa flatbread. Miso ice cream. Zucchini pizzas. White bean meatball subs. Avocado waffles. And many more.

Guess what you won't find in my recipes?

Expensive lengthy ingredient lists, multiple complex recipe steps, and mysterious ingredients that are hard to find.

And the results are delicious as well as help meet daily nutritional quotas.

MY RECIPES HAVE ONLY 4 INGREDIENTS

Inspired by my family, my all-too-busy life, as well as my friendly blog and Instagram community, my first goal when outlining my book was to keep the ingredient list down. Way down. Many recipes on my blog already have few ingredients, but for this book, I went further and stuck to the rule that each recipe would have only 4 ingredients. Why 4? To make eating healthier insanely easier.

It is my hope that you have or will build out your own healthy *capsule pantry* so you have ingredients at your fingertips, or that you memorize the few ingredients needed for your favorite recipe(s) in the book and stand ready to grab them on a whim at the grocery store.

I also hope many of these become your back-pocket recipes, either stand-alone or as foundations for more complex creations, customized by you.

MY RECIPES HELP YOU EAT MORE PLANTS

You don't have to be adhering to any specific diet to enjoy these recipes. The recipes themselves use plant-based, less-processed ingredients that are dairy-free, gluten-free, refined-sugar-free, with nut-free options. While they are suitable for vegan and vegetarian diets, often for paleo, and sometimes keto diets, they are also useful to anyone who simply wants to eat more vegetables, less processed foods, and foods without dairy, meat, and less refined sugar.

Since you are reading this book, you probably already know that public health organizations are increasingly promoting the wisdom of eating more plant-based foods and less processed foods to support overall health.

Not all the ingredients used in this book are unprocessed. A few are canned or packaged, including pumpkin puree, beans, shredded coconut, and quality dark chocolate. I often provide purchase guidance on how to choose the healthiest versions, and live links to recommended brands can be found on my book resource page on my website here: greensmoothiegourmet.com/resources-for-crazy-healthy-with-4-ingredients/. There, I also provide scientific studies that indicate sometimes a canned or processed option can be nutritionally wise.

MY RECIPES TARGET 8 NUTRITIONAL AREAS

Another plus of this book is that it is structured so you can quickly choose the recipe that supports a specific nutritional need. There are six chapters, defined by food type, so named:

Clean Chocolate Treats
Speedy Morning Meals
Easy Cakes & Cookies
Nutritious Sides & Snacks
Healthy Pops & Ice Cream
Nourishing & Hydrating Drinks

Within each of those chapters, you will find 8 recipes, each with 1 or more ingredient that supports a specific and popular nutritional category, including:

1. Protein & Fiber
2. Energizer & Brain Support
3. Immunity & Detox
4. Good Mood Food & Stress-Reducer
5. Sleep Support
6. Weight-Control & Workout Food
7. Hair, Skin & Nail Support
8. Anti-Inflammatories (paperback)

The reasons behind the supporting ingredient are discussed in each recipe introduction. Tips and swaps are also provided, and each recipe has a final image so you can see what you are making.

INGREDIENTS THAT DON'T COUNT AS ONE OF THE 4

None of the 4 ingredients in each recipe is another recipe within the book. I also don't count water, salt or pepper, or coating for cookware as ingredients. Within the recipe instructions, I'll note when you need water, but I suggest you add salt and pepper according to your own taste. A pinch of quality sea salt to most recipes accentuates the flavors.

MY RECIPES ARE SMALL BATCH & USE MINIMAL EQUIPMENT

All my recipes are written for small batch cooking to give you a chance to try without using up a lot of time and ingredients. But of course they are easy to double and triple when the need arises. My recipes also require minimal equipment, such as a blender or a food processor, common tools and pans.

WHERE TO FIND MY INGREDIENTS AND EQUIPMENT

Additionally, all of the ingredients and equipment I used for these recipes can be found at general grocery store chains, Target, Cosco, Whole Foods, Trader Joes, and on Amazon. On my blog, on my book resources page, you can find a current list of the ingredients and equipment I used in my recipes. I also provide current links to nutritional studies to support the nutritional information in my recipes. Finally, at the end of this book, you will find my *capsule pantry* guide to aid you in stocking your own pantry with healthy ingredients you need to make these recipes and your own versions.

MY ROAD TO NUTRITIONAL CHOICES

Actually, my interest in clean eating began in my college days.
I was in an accelerated biology/biochemistry degree program and the long hard hours of study and poor eating began to take a toll. One particular November, I failed an organic chemistry test because I simply hadn't had the mental energy to memorize all those formulas. That academic failure was my trigger - I had only two choices, start eating right or fail.
I changed my eating choices overnight, and, soon, it became common to see me pull out a raw carrot to munch or stir up a jar of chilled overnight oats, or pop a homemade chocolate nut butter cup.
To give my friends credit, at first they regarded me as an oddity, but it didn't take them long to trade in their unhealthy takeout for fresh salads and quick chia cups. And an understanding of the benefits of veganism to body and planet

quickly followed. Now I'm finding my college biology and biochemistry knowledge comes in handy in healthy recipe creation - cooking, after all, really is chemistry. Contact me on Instagram at @greensmoothiegourmet, or by comments on my blog recipe posts at greensmoothiegourmet.com . I am always happy to see and share remakes of my recipes, and hear about your experiences or recommendations!

Dee xx

Clean Chocolate Treats

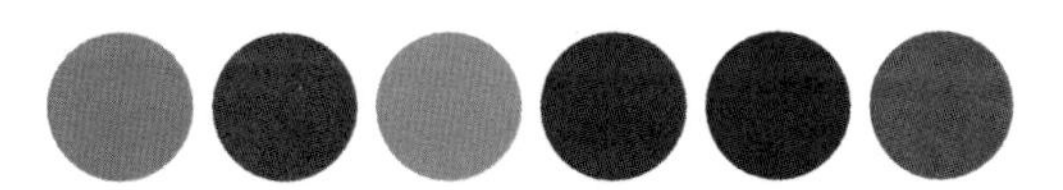

Lentil Chocolate Fudge Cups

It is not every day an easy-to-make treat is high in protein, fiber and is made from a normally-savory ingredient like lentils. These chocolate-y sweet treats melt in your mouth like the unhealthiest of fudge, yet they are far more nutritious. High in slow-absorbing fiber from lentil flour and flax, and rich in protein from almond butter. Lentil flour is easy to make, just put uncooked lentil beans in a food processor or coffee grinder.

MAKES 8 MINI CUPS

1/4 cup lentil flour
1/2 cup almond butter
1/2 cup dark chocolate chips
1 tbsp ground flax seeds

CLEAN
CHOCOLATE TREATS

Protein & Fiber

PREPARATION

1. Line a mini-cupcake pan with 8 paper liners. Melt the chocolate in a heat-safe measuring cup in a microwave for 60 seconds or by sitting the cup in a pot of just boiled hot water. Stir until all is melted.
2. Put 1 tbsp of melted chocolate mixture into each cup and use a spoon to drag chocolate up the sides to create a chocolate cup. Put the pan in refrigerator to set.
3. Make lentil flour by processing 1/2 cup any color in a food processor or coffee grinder until it reaches the texture of flour.
4. In a bowl, stir together the flour, butter, flax seeds and 4 tbsp of melted chocolate. You want a sticky batter so add more melted chocolate if your mixture is crumbly.
5. Roll 1 tbsp of that mixture into balls, press flat and insert into cups. Spoon the rest of the melted chocolate on top. Sprinkle with toppings such as crushed nuts or salt flakes. Refrigerate until set, about 1 hour.
6. Keep these cups in a sealed container in the refrigerator or freezer.

protein 5 fiber 2 fat 4.4 calories 81 sugars 4.4 carbs 9

SWAPS, BOOSTS & SOURCES

Not ready to make lentil flour? Use almond flour or oat flour instead. Use sunflower seed butter to make it nut-free. Quality dark chocolate is at least 70% cacao and has minimal ingredients. Find links to ingredients, equipment, and studies at: greensmoothiegourmet.com/resources/

Quinoa Chocolate Brittle

Quinoa is your brain's best friend - this gluten-free pseudo-cereal is one of the few plant foods that provide a complete protein, all nine amino acids needed to process the brain's essential neurotransmitters. It's easy to prepare popped or toasted, just rinse and dry saute in a pan on the stove. Then mix that quinoa with your favorite nut butter and energizing melted dark chocolate to make an easy brittle powerful enough to lift you through your day.

MAKES 10 SHARDS

3/4 cup quinoa, popped
1 1/2 cup dark chocolate chips or bar
3 tbsp almond butter
1/4 cup maple syrup

CLEAN
CHOCOLATE TREATS

Energizer &
Brain Support

PREPARATION

1. Line an 8x4-inch loaf pan with parchment paper.
2. Pop the quinoa. To do this, first rinse uncooked quinoa in a strainer to remove the bitter coating, nature's natural seed protectant. Then dry saute it in a deep pot. As it heats, stir continually and you will hear popping, though not as dramatically as popcorn. Once the popping ceases and the quinoa smells nutty and is slightly browned (about 1-2 minutes), pour the popped quinoa into a mixing bowl.
3. To the bowl, add the maple syrup and almond butter. Stir until well combined.
4. Spread the sticky quinoa mixture on to the bottom of the lined loaf pan. Use a spoon to level the surface.
5. Melt the chocolate in a heat-safe measuring cup in a microwave for 60 seconds or by sitting the cup in a pot of just boiled hot water. Stir until all is melted. Pour melted chocolate on top of quinoa layer. Refrigerate until set, about 4 hours.
6. Dip a long sharp knife into boiling water, wipe it dry and use the hot knife to cut slices. Store refrigerated.

protein 4 fiber 1 fat 8 calories 181 sugars 14 carbs 26

SWAPS, BOOSTS & SOURCES

Make it nut-free by swapping nut butter for sunflower seed butter. Amaranth, another healthy pseudo-grain, can be popped and used similarly to quinoa here. Find current links to the ingredients and equipment I used, and nutritional studies at: greensmoothiegourmet.com/resources/

Tahini Cookie Dough Bricks

Tahini, a buttery paste made of pure sesame seeds, is known as a strong immune system booster. But it has more hidden talents, including the ability to balance hormones, repair tissues, keep skin elastic and youthful. In these easy-to-prep squares, tahini provides a nutty balance to chocolate chips, and a creamy melt-in-your-mouth texture. Find quality tahini butter in the peanut butter area of your grocery store.

MAKES 16 (1-INCH) BRICKS

1/4 cup tahini (unsweetened sesame seed butter)
2/3 (15oz can) garbanzo beans/chickpeas (organic, BPA-free)
1/4 cup maple syrup
1/3 cup dark chocolate chips

PREPARATION

1. Line a 4-inch square pan with parchment paper. (to double recipe, use loaf pan)
2. Open a can of cooked chickpeas, rinse and drain. Measure out 1 cup of chickpeas. Measure out a 1/4 cup of tahini, try to avoid the oil if you have a runny brand.
3. Blend or process chickpeas and tahini until smooth. Add the maple syrup a tablespoon at a time until you have a formable batter texture. Depending on your tahini brand, that might need less maple syrup than 1/4 cup. Add a tbsp or two of coconut flour if you have to dry out the dough further.
4. Fold in chocolate chips.
5. Press dough into pan, and smoothie surface with back of a spoon.
6. Freeze pan for 1 hour or until solid enough to slice with a knife dipped in hot water.
7. Store in an airtight container in the refrigerator for several weeks, or frozen for several months.

protein 5.9 fiber 8.2 fat 10.8 calories 227 sugars 17 carbs 30.3

SWAPS, BOOSTS & SOURCES

Tahini, which is sesame seed butter, can be swapped for a nut or another seed butter. Be sure to use a quality tahini with only sesame seeds in the ingredients. Add a tsp of baobab powder or camu camu powder to dramatically boost the immunity power. Find current links to the ingredients and equipment I used, and nutritional studies at: greensmoothiegourmet.com/resources/

Caramel Apple Chocolate Pops

Caramel apples are the festive icon of carnivals and amusement parks. The flavorful hard-candy-coating challenges the jawbone, but not this healthier version. These apple slices are perched on lollipop sticks, slathered with date paste, and dipped in dark chocolate. Each pop provides fiber from the fresh apple, iron from dates, and mood-enhancing effects flavanols and magnesium from dark chocolate. So have a healthy caramel apple and smile.

MAKES 6-8 POPS

2 fresh apples (grannysmith or gala)

1/2 cup date paste (5 dates, soaked & pitted + 1/4 cup water)

1/2 cup dark chocolate chips or bar

Toppings: maple syrup, nuts, chocolate chips, sprinkles

CLEAN
CHOCOLATE TREATS

Good Mood Food
& Stress Reducer

PREPARATION

1. Make the date paste. Soak dates overnight, pit them, and blend with water until smooth.
2. Line a cookie sheet with parchment paper.
3. Wash and slice the apples. Cut 2 uniform, thick slices from each side of the apple core. Chop leftover apple and eat as a snack.
4. Insert a lollipop or popsicle stick into each slice. Spread date paste on one side of each.
5. Melt the chocolate in a heat-safe measuring cup in a microwave for 60 seconds or by sitting the cup in a pot of just boiled hot water. Stir until all is melted.
6. Dip the apples one by one into the melted chocolate. Spin the apple slice a few times and hold each in the air until coating seems solid. Then set the apple slice down on the parchment, date paste side up.
7. Sprinkle each coated caramel apple slice with toppings, such as sprinkles, or crushed nuts or seeds for more protein.
8. Store completed pops on a parchment-lined pan in refrigerator for up to two days.

protein 1.2 fiber 2.6 fat 6 calories 111 sugars 10.3 carbs 14

SWAPS, BOOSTS & SOURCES

Use nut butter or sunflower seed butter instead of making date paste. It's not 'caramel', but still delicious. Find current links to the ingredients and equipment I used, and nutritional studies at: greensmoothiegourmet.com/resources/

Snow Capped Kiwi Chips

Kiwi is bursting with sleep-supporting serotonin, so it is not surprising that eaten regularly, this juicy green fruit can help you sleep faster, longer, and better. Dipped here in coconut butter only enhances the sleep support capabilities of this snack. Coconut butter is so rich and nutrient-dense, it is often used as a cleaner substitute for traditional white chocolate.

MAKES 12 CHIPS

4 kiwi, peeled and chopped

1/2 cup coconut butter (homemade or bought)

CLEAN
CHOCOLATE TREATS

Sleep Support

PREPARATION

1. Add a sheet of parchment to a quarter cookie sheet, and top with a cooling rack.
2. Peel and slice 4 kiwis into 3-5 slices, depending on the size of your fruit.
3. If you want to make homemade coconut butter, add 1 cup shredded coconut, unsweetened, to a high-speed blender. Blend the coconut until it turns to butter, in a few minutes.
4. If you intend to use store-bought coconut butter, uncover jar and put it in a pot of boiling water. Stir and chop until it is melted, about 3-4 minutes as well.
5. Once your coconut butter is liquid either way and ready for dipping, dip each kiwi and set it on the rack to set. Store for one day in the refrigerator.

protein 1 fiber 2.4 fat 6.1 calories 77 sugars 2.9 carbs 6

SWAPS, BOOSTS & SOURCES

The kiwi is essential here to support sleep. You can also dip the kiwi into melted chocolate but beware, of course, chocolate eaten at night may interfere with sleep. Find current links to the ingredients and equipment I used, and nutritional studies at: greensmoothiegourmet.com/resources/

Ginger Butter Mousse

This creamy mousse has bright sparks of ginger and is airy from aquafaba. Fresh ginger root speeds up the metabolism, which aids in weight-loss, especially targeting belly fat. Cacao butter - also called cocoa butter - is blond, part of a raw chocolate bean and is a highly nutritious whole food. Here it also lends a buttery, white chocolate flavor to this fresh mousse.

MAKES 3 SERVINGS

3/4 cup aquafaba (liquid from 2 chickpea cans)

2 tsp fresh ginger

1/2 cup nut butter (or sunflower seed butter)

2 tbsp cacao butter, melted

PREPARATION

1. Open 2 cans of garbanzo beans/chickpeas or white beans, pour off the liquid, measuring out 3/4 cup. Each 15oz can typically yields 1/2 cup of aquafaba. Refrigerate the beans and remaining aquafaba for another use.
2. Prepare the fresh ginger. First peel a knob or two, and then cut into small chunks. Crush chunks in a garlic press until you have 2 tsp of ginger pulp.
3. Melt the cacao butter by putting it in a heat-safe measuring cup that is sitting in just boiled water.
4. Add the aquafaba to a mixing bowl, and use a hand-mixer to whip it into a fluffy texture. This can take between 7-10 minutes. If you own a stand-mixer, use that for convenience.
5. Once whipped, fold together the aquafaba, nut butter and melted cacao butter in a bowl. Stir or whisk the mixture until smooth. Taste-test and add 1 tsp of ginger, stir it in and taste-test again and decide if you want to add the second tsp of ginger. You also might want to add 1-2 tsp of maple syrup if you need it to be sweeter.
6. Pour the mousse into small glasses and refrigerate until ready to serve.
7. Serve as is or top with whipped cream or cinnamon just prior to serving.

protein 2 fiber 0.4 fat 1.8 calories 74 sugars 8 carbs 14

CLEAN
CHOCOLATE TREATS

Workout Food &
Weight Control

SWAPS, BOOSTS & SOURCES

Drop the spare tsp of ginger in 1/2 cup of water to make 2 ginger shots if you choose not to use it in this mousse. Find current links to the ingredients and equipment I used, and nutritional studies at: greensmoothiegourmet.com/resources/

Chocolate Tocos Cookies

No-bake recipes are a gift from the freezer gods, and this high-fiber no-bake cookie recipe is a gift to the body's metabolism. Coconut flour is key to giving a no-bake recipe a cake-like texture, and nutritionally, adds quality fat and fiber, essential to many body processes. The date paste and cacao are both nutrient-dense but it is the tocos powder that specifically supports the health of hair, skin and nails.

MAKES 9 COOKIES

3/4 cup coconut flour

1/4 cup date paste (4 dates, soaked & pitted + 3 tbsp water)

2 tbsp cacao powder

1 tbsp tocos powder

CLEAN CHOCOLATE TREATS

Hair, Skin & Nail Support

PREPARATION

1. Line a quarter cookie sheet with parchment paper.
2. Soak dates overnight, pit them and blend with water until smooth.
3. In a bowl, stir together the flour, date paste, cacao powder and tocos powder until fully incorporated into a dough. Depending on the size and moisture in your dates, you may have to add a bit more flour or water until dough is formable, but not sticking to fingers.
4. Freeze the dough for 30 minutes to make it easier to handle.
5. Press 2 tbsp of dough into a 2-inch cookie cutter directly on the cookie sheet. Repeat until you have 9 cookies. Freeze for 1 hour.
6. Optional toppings: Either leave cookies plain, or melt dark chocolate chips and dip the cookies half-way.
7. Store cookies in an airtight container in the freezer for 2 months.

protein 1.5 fiber 1.9 fat 2.1 calories 34 sugars 2.4 carbs 5.5

SWAPS, BOOSTS & SOURCES

Not interested in using tocos powder? Then substitute any protein powder or even more almond flour in equal measure. Find current links to the ingredients and equipment I used, and nutritional studies at: greensmoothiegourmet.com/resources/

Chocolate Orange Turmeric Cups

Turmeric is a spice that we now know is super powerful at controlling inflammation, a key to avoiding disease and staying healthy. Add in chocolates and oranges and you have a powerful chocolate treat with high ORAC values, which indicates the ability for the food to devour body-damaging free radicals. Chocolate, oranges, almonds and turmeric actually have some of the highest ORAC values of any food.

MAKES 9 MINI CUPS

1 cup dark chocolate chips or bar
2 tbsp orange juice, fresh
1/2 cup almond butter
1/2 tsp turmeric, ground

CLEAN
CHOCOLATE TREATS

Anti-Inflammatory

PREPARATION

1. Line a mini-cupcake pan with 9 paper liners.
2. In a heat-safe measuring cup, melt the almond butter gently, either by microwave in intervals of 15 seconds, or via hot water bath, setting the cup in a pot of just-boiled hot water.
3. Add the orange juice and keep stirring until the butter is smooth.
4. Add in the turmeric and stir until incorporated.
5. Melt the chocolate in a heat-safe measuring cup in a microwave for 60 seconds or by sitting the cup in a pot of just boiled hot water. Stir until all is melted.
6. Assemble the cups by filling them about 1/3 of the way with the chocolate mixture. Then set pan in freezer for 5 minutes. Spoon on the nut butter mixture, then set in freezer for 10 minutes. Finally pour on the top chocolate layer and let set in freezer for 5 minutes.
7. Serve with a dusting of orange peel or cinnamon. Keep refrigerated for 1 week or freeze for 2 months.

protein 1.2 fiber 1.9 fat 6.1 calories 108 sugars 10.2 carbs 12

SWAPS, BOOSTS & SOURCES

Turmeric can be left out. Swap almond butter with any nut or seed butter. Find current links to the ingredients and equipment I used, and nutritional studies at: greensmoothiegourmet.com/resources/

Speedy Morning Meals

Granola Quinoa Breakfast Pizza
protein & fiber - page 37

Apple Baked Donuts
energizer & brain support - page 39

Chocolate Gingerbread Milk
immunity & detox - page 41

Savory Avocado Waffle
good mood food & stress reducer - page 43

Oat Cherry Breakfast Bars
sleep support - page 45

Potato Cauliflower Tots
weight control & workout food - page 47

5-Minute Homemade Hummus
hair, skin & nail support - page 49

Lemon Cashew Yogurt
anti-inflammatory

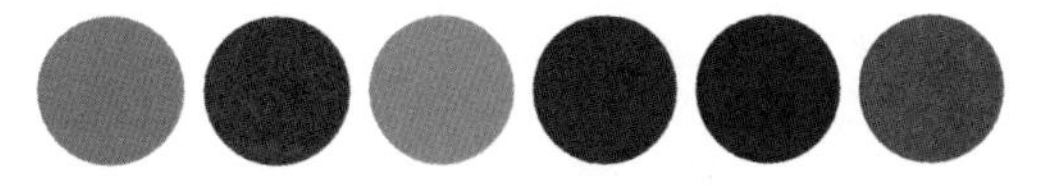

Granola Quinoa Breakfast Pizza

Eating pizza for breakfast is not new, but instead of a cold slice of tomato-sauce pizza from the previous night, how about a protein-rich granola breakfast pizza with yogurt and fruits of a variety only limited by your imagination. Quinoa, as you know, is one of nature's only plant-based sources of complete protein, and cooking or blending doesn't change the nutritional value. Good Morning!

MAKES ONE 6-INCH ROUND PIZZA

1 cup granola + toasted quinoa
1 tbsp cacao powder
2 tbsp coconut oil, melted
2 tbsp maple syrup

SPEEDY
MORNING MEALS
-
Protein & Fiber

PREPARATION

1. Line the bottom of a 6-inch round tart pan with round parchment paper to fit.
2. Dry-saute raw quinoa in a saucepan over medium heat. Toast, stirring about 2 minutes until the quinoa is slightly browned and smells nutty. Add this to your favorite granola.
3. To a large mixing bowl, add the granola/quinoa mixture, cacao powder, coconut oil, and maple syrup. Stir until combined.
4. Press the mixture into the pan, pushing up the sides to create a pie crust. Set the pie crust in the freezer for at least two hours or even overnight. Top it when you are ready to eat.
5. I topped my breakfast crust with yogurt, fruit and seeds. Feel free to top it with your favorite breakfast foods.

protein 3.4 fiber 2.3 fat 7.5 calories 56 sugars 6.1 carbs 13.9

SWAPS, BOOSTS & SOURCES

Swap the cacao powder for pumpkin pie spices, and apples to the fruit toppings for a spicy fall-flavors crust. I also topped mine with incredibly powerful mood-boosters, goji berries. Find current links to the ingredients and equipment I used, and nutritional studies at: greensmoothiegourmet.com/resources/

Apple Baked Donuts

Apples have super-powers regarding brain healthy, especially protective of brain tissue damage, and highly supportive of an important brain neurotransmitter, acetylcholine, which can decline with age. Add in the extra-ordinary antioxidant powers and high-fiber, apples are a nutritious addition to these donuts. The yogurt provides protein and gut-health support, and the flax seeds add a boatload of nutrients. Happy dunking.

MAKES 12 DONUTS

2 cups self-rising flour
3/4 cup apple puree (or applesauce)
1 cup yogurt
2 flax seed eggs (2 tbsp flax seed + 6 tbsp water)

SPEEDY MORNING MEALS

Energizer & Brain Support

PREPARATION

1. In a large mixing bowl, make flax seed egg by mixing 2 tbsp ground flax seed with 6 tbsp of water and letting it sit for 10 minutes. Rub a donut pan lightly with oil.
2. Peel and core two large apples (I used Gala), and puree to a creamy texture in a high-speed blender. Add a tablespoon of water if necessary, to help it blend. Or use quality unsweetened applesauce.
3. When flax seed eggs are ready, add to the bowl the flour, 3/4 cup apple puree (or applesauce), yogurt and 1/4 cup water, then mix with a hand mixer until dough is just batter-like.
4. Either spoon the batter into the donut pan rings, or pipe it using a tip-less frosting piping bag. Tap the pan on the counter so levels of batter are even.
5. Bake the donuts at 350 F for 15 minutes or until a tester comes out clean.
6. Coat the donuts with a dusting of cinnamon sugar, which is 2 tbsp cinnamon + 1/2 cup coconut palm sugar, a plant-based brown sugar.

protein 3.6 fiber 1.1 fat 0.8 calories 103 sugars 3.1 carbs 19.4

SWAPS, BOOSTS & SOURCES

Use unsweetened, low fat yogurt. I used coconut but any type should work. Self-rising flour is made of all-purpose flour, baking powder and salt, so it is a perfect to simplify the ingredient list. However, it is not highly nutritious. For more nutrition but denser texture, substitute oat flour, adding 2 tsp baking powder and a pinch of salt. Find current links to the ingredients and equipment I used, and nutritional studies at: greensmoothiegourmet.com/resources/

Chocolate Gingerbread Milk

Cinnamon is incredibly powerful at detoxing and immunity support. It can prevent cavities, fight allergies, even support blood pressure levels. Molasses contributes immunity-supportive choline as well as glutathione, a strong antioxidant that fights infections. Cacao powder is raw chocolate that boosts immunity by contributing nutrients the body needs to mount an immune defense, including iron, zinc, selenium, and vitamin A.

MAKES 2 CUPS MILK

2 cups almond milk (or your favorite)
2 tbsp cacao powder
1 tbsp light molasses (or maple syrup)
Spices (1 tsp ginger; 1 tbsp cinnamon; 1/2 tsp nutmeg; pinch of clove; pinch of black pepper)

PREPARATION

1. Blend up milk, cacao powder, spices and molasses. Feel free to use pumpkin pie spice instead of all the individual spices above; it is not exact but close.
2. Serve chilled, perhaps with a cinnamon sprinkle.
3. Store the milk in the refrigerator for 3 days.

(1/2 cup) protein 2.5 fiber 3.2 fat 3.3 calories 70 sugars 5.8 carbs 12.7

SWAPS, BOOSTS & SOURCES

You can use blackstrap molasses instead of light for the added nutrition, but you'll have to taste-test and add maple syrup as well since blackstrap molasses can be bitter.
Find current links to the ingredients and equipment I used, and nutritional studies at: greensmoothiegourmet.com/resources/

Savory Avocado Waffle

These are savory waffles that can be topped with veggies or unsweetened yogurt or even an avocado spread. Oats boost serotonin production which combats stress, enhances learning, and memory function. And avocado supports every single body process, keeping you full and sugar balanced. Both ingredients provide stress-management with a myriad of nutrients that boost energy levels and mood.

MAKES 3 SMALL WAFFLES

1/4 cup oat flour (gluten-free)

1/2 avocado

1/4 cup +2 tbsp milk

1/2 tsp baking powder

SPEEDY
MORNING MEALS

Good Mood Food
& Stress Reducer

PREPARATION

1. Into a 2-cup measuring cup, add the ingredients and using a hand-mixer, quickly blend up batter.
2. Turn on your waffle iron and heat according to the machine's instructions.
3. Pour the waffle batter into your waffle iron and cook according to your machine's instructions.
4. I used a mini waffle maker, called a Mini Dash. I cooked each waffle for 4 minutes to allow them to have an exterior crust and be cooked within. This recipe made 3 mini waffles.
5. I serve these topped with tomatoes, olives and a sprinkling of parsley. Consider adding nutritional yeast, parsley, scallions, and of course salt and pepper.

protein 2.3 fiber 3 fat 7.5 calories 109 sugars 1.1 carbs 9.1

SWAPS, BOOSTS & SOURCES

It is fine to swap the flour for all purpose flour in case that is all you have on hand. These waffles are not sweet, more neutral, a healthy platform for savory toppings. Find current links to the ingredients and equipment I used, and nutritional studies at: greensmoothiegourmet.com/resources/

Oat Cherry Breakfast Bars

Healthy sleep is influenced heavily by the right balance of protein and fats early in the day to kick off metabolism, and trigger melatonin at bedtime. This bar fits the bill! The oats provide calcium and magnesium which promote quality sleep, cashew butter provides protein, and the cherries set the stage for your body to make melatonin later when you are ready to sleep.

MAKES 4 BARS

1/2 cup gluten-free rolled oats
1/2 cup apple sauce
1/4 cup cashew butter
1/4 cup dried cherries

PREPARATION

1. Line a 4-inch square pan with parchment paper. If you are doubling the recipe, use an 8x4-inch loaf pan.
2. In a large bowl, stir together the oats, sauce, butter, and cherries. Taste-test for sweetness; add 1 tbsp maple syrup if you want the mixture sweeter.
3. Press this mixture into the pan, using the back of a spoon to flatten the surface.
4. Set the pan in the freezer for about two hours or even overnight to solidify the mixture.
5. When you are ready to slice, dip your knife in a pot of boiling water, wipe it dry and cut into 2-inch square pieces.
6. Store the bars in a covered container in the refrigerator for about 4 days. Freeze for 3 months.

protein 3.8 fiber 2.2 fat 7.7 calories 163 sugars 9 carbs 21.3

SWAPS, BOOSTS & SOURCES

Swap out the cashew butter for sunflower seed butter to make this nut-free. Other possible add-ins include sunflower seeds, raisins, cranberries, cinnamon. Find current links to the ingredients and equipment I used, and nutritional studies at: greensmoothiegourmet.com/resources/

Potato Cauliflower Tots

These veggie-filled tater tots make a delicious savory breakfast and are a powerful weight-loss tool. The reason is they contain white potatoes and white potatoes, when chilled, convert to "resistant starch." Resistant starch "resists" digestion which carries many benefits including prolonged feelings of fullness, all of which supports weight control. Resistant starch also supports a healthy gut,, and even boosts in immunity. This energizing breakfast should be made the prior night, refrigerated, and eaten chilled in the morning to fully support weight control.

MAKES15 TOTS

1 cup white potato (cooked, peeled)
3/4 cup cauliflower, chopped + steamed
1/4 cup green onion, chopped
1/4 cup chickpea crumbs (or panko or breadcrumbs)

SPEEDY
MORNING MEALS

Weight Control &
Workout Food

PREPARATION

1. Heat the oven to 400 F. Line a baking sheet with parchment paper. Chop green onion.
2. Steam the cauliflower, then chop or crumble it in a food processor. Put the cauliflower in a strainer, and press moisture out using the back of a spoon. Put the cauliflower (back) in the food processor. (you can also use store-bought riced cauliflower, found in your grocer freezer section.)
3. Bake the potato either by baking in the oven or in the microwave (poke with holes, wrap in a paper towel, microwave 7 minutes). Peel and put white potato in food processor.
4. Add to the food processor, the onion and crumbs, and pulse mixture until crumbly. Use your hands to make 1-inch long oval tot shapes.
5. Line them up on the pan and bake 25-35 minutes or until outside is crispy.
6. You can, of course, eat these hot. But if you want the weight-loss effect, you'll need to let the dish cool to room temperature; then refrigerate covered overnight.
7. Serve cold for breakfast, with refined-sugar-free ketchup.

protein 1.7 fiber 1.3 fat 0.2 calories 18 sugars 0.6 carbs 3.3

SWAPS, BOOSTS & SOURCES

Increase flavor with garlic powder, oregano, basil to taste. Swap white potatoes for sweet potatoes to reduce the glycemic index, however this will not provide the weight-control tactic as sweet potatoes don't convert to resistant starch. Find current links to the ingredients and equipment I used, and nutritional studies at: greensmoothiegourmet.com/resources/

5-Minute Homemade Hummus

Controlling inflammation is one key to staying healthy, and strongly supports hair, skin and nails. Foods that fight inflammation often have a high ORAC value, the ability to devour body-damaging free radicals. Hummus, a spread made from chickpeas, tahini, garlic and lemon juice, is generally a high ORAC food. Just 1/2 cup of this recipe has an ORAC value of 3980. The USDA recommends ingesting 3000-5000 ORAC units per day for optimum health.

MAKES 1 CUP

1 (15oz can) garbanzo beans/chickpeas (organic, BPA-free)
1/3 cup tahini (unsweetened sesame seed butter)
4 garlic cloves, crushed
1/4 cup lemon juice

PREPARATION

1. Make your own hummus. It only takes five minutes. Drain the beans but save the liquid in the refrigerator for 3-4 days and use in another recipe, for instance the ginger mousse or the aquafaba apple cake, both recipes in this book.
2. Blend up all ingredients, adding a bit of water to increase a creamy texture.
3. Store covered and refrigerated.

(1/4 cup) protein 18 fiber 15 fat 15.4 calories 396 sugars 8.5 carbs 50.1

SWAPS, BOOSTS & SOURCES

Customize your hummus by adding parsley or kalamata olives or red peppers or basil, all high ORAC foods. Find current links to the ingredients and equipment I used, and nutritional studies at: greensmoothiegourmet.com/resources/

Lemon Cashew Yogurt

Lemon yogurt is the perfect anti-inflammatory. Citrus fruits are fierce inflammation fighters, with high levels of vitamins C and E, and loads of antioxidants great at neutralizing free radicals that cause illness. Cashews are high in omega-3 fatty acids that lower inflammation. Here, I spread this fresh homemade yogurt on watermelon pizza slices. Watermelon is also an incredibly strong anti-inflammatory, and holds other qualities that support muscle soreness, fight disease, and heart health.

MAKES 2 CUPS

2 cups cashews (raw, unsalted)
2 quality probiotics capsules
3 tbsp fresh lemon juice
pinch of sea salt

PREPARATION

1. To prep for this recipe, clean blender jar, measuring cups, mixing bowl and stirring tools with soap and very hot water to prevent bacteria growth. Juice the lemons, strain out seeds.
2. Rinse the cashews and put in a measuring cup full of water in the refrigerator overnight. The next day, drain, rinse and put cashews in a blender along with 1 cup of water and the lemon juice. Blend until creamy.
3. Pour the mixture into a mixing bowl, break open each probiotics capsule and pour their powder into the bowl.
4. Stir all ingredients, using a wooden spoon since metal will damage the probiotics.
5. Cover the bowl with a paper towel or cheesecloth and store at room temperature for 12 hours in a corner of your counter or other non-sunny area.
6. After 6 hours, stir the yogurt, put it into a covered container and refrigerate. Let it chill and thicken for two hours. Then it is ready to eat. The yogurt can last 3 days.
7. To make a watermelon pizza, slice a watermelon, insert popsicle sticks, top with your favorite spreads or yogurt and top with fruits!

(1/2 cup) protein 10.6 fiber 2.1 fat 31.8 calories 396 sugars 3.7 carbs 22.6

SWAPS, BOOSTS & SOURCES

Swap lemon for lime juice. Add baobab powder, a citrus-flavored powerful immunity booster made from the crushed root of a baobab tree. Find current links to the ingredients and equipment I used, and nutritional studies at: greensmoothiegourmet.com/resources/

Easy Cakes & Cookies

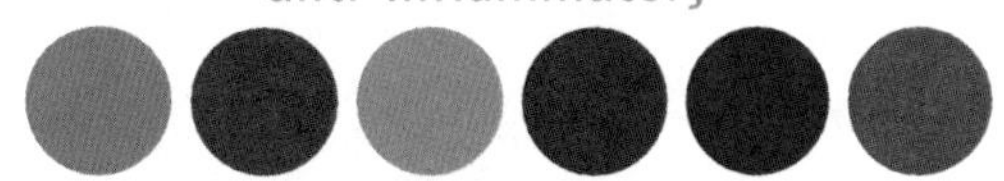

Apple Aquafaba Cake

Apples are more than a fruit - they are a memory of childhood, of home, of family, of holidays, of spices. So is cake. They come together in this simple yet healthy recipe that yields a delicate sweet cake suitable for tea, snack, dessert, or gift-giving. The texture is so incredible with only four ingredients, that I think there must be a fifth ingredient: magic.

MAKES 1 (3X6) MINI LOAF OR 2 MUFFINS

1 medium (sweet) apple, peeled and chunked
1/4 cup organic cane sugar
1/2 cup all purpose flour
2 faux eggs (aquafaba - 6 tbsp liquid from chickpea can)

EASY
CAKES & COOKIES

Protein & Fiber

PREPARATION

1. Coat 1 mini-loaf pan (6x3-inch) with vegan butter and a dusting of flour or line two cupcake tins.
2. Preheat oven to 400 F. Peel apples, chop into small chunks.
3. Prepare the two "faux" aquafaba eggs by opening a can of chickpeas (13.5oz) organic and BPA-free and reserving the liquid. That is your aquafaba; refrigerate the chickpeas for other uses. Into a large mixing bowl, spoon 3 tbsp of room-temperature aquafaba per each egg needed - in this recipe, we need 2 eggs, so spoon 6 tbsp into the bowl.
4. Into the bowl, add the sugar and use a hand-mixer to combine. Slowly add flour, mixing thoroughly after each addition. Hand-fold apple chunks into batter.
5. Pour the batter into equal measure into the loaf pan or split between two cupcake liners.
6. Bake at 400 F for 10 minutes, then lower heat to 350 F and bake for another 30 minutes, testing with a clean stick after 20 minutes. The top should be golden. The last bake might be slightly less for muffins.

protein 1.9 fiber 3.3 fat 0.8 calories 182 sugars 20.5 carbs 42.6

SWAPS, BOOSTS & SOURCES

You can double and triple recipe, but make each batch individually - aquafaba works best as an egg replacer when it is asked to replace no more than two eggs at a time. Find current links to the ingredients and equipment I used, and nutritional studies at: greensmoothiegourmet.com/resources/

2-ingredient Sugar Cookies

Yes, you can make a cookie using only two ingredients. Almond flour plus maple syrup has the perfect combination of protein and fat to carry the day. Be sure to chill the dough before baking and bake at a low heat so they don't burn. Then, dip them in chocolate. Or sprinkle with sugar. Or make superfood sandwich cookies. Mix in superfoods chocolate (cacao powder), pitaya (pink), matcha (green), blue spirulina (blue), to boost nutrition.

MAKES 18-24 COOKIES

1 cup almond flour
1/4 cup maple syrup

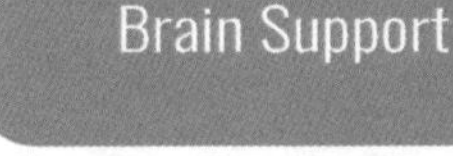

PREPARATION

1. Preheat oven to 250 F. Yes, 250 F. These cookies need to bake at low heat. Line a one-quarter cookie sheet with parchment.
2. In a large bowl, stir or hand-mix together the flour and maple syrup until you have a malleable cookie dough texture.
3. To change flavors, choose to add 1/2 tsp of cacao powder for chocolate, or of pitaya powder, or of matcha powder, and or of blue spirulina. Taste-test each for sweetness, adding a touch more maple syrup if needed. Adjust texture with more flour or more syrup if you need it dryer or wetter to reach cookie dough texture.
4. Wrap the dough in parchment paper and freeze for 15 minutes. On the parchment-lined pan, press 1-2 tbsp of dough into a round cookie cutter. OR lay another sheet of parchment paper on top and roll it out about 1/4-inch to 1/2-inch thick. Use cookie cutters to cut shapes, then pick away dough between shapes, roll that, cut and repeat. One-inch star cutters gave me 24 cookies.
5. Either way, bake cookies for 20-25 minutes or until you see they are browning. Remove pan, and cool. To dip with chocolate, first freeze cooled cookies 15 minutes then dip in chocolate chips melted in microwave at 60 seconds. Or sprinkle cookies with sugar, first dampening tops with a dab of water.
6. Store cookies in sealed container at room temperature. Or freeze batter or cookies.

(1 cookie) protein 4 fiber 1 fat 2 calories 18 sugars 2 carbs 3

SWAPS, BOOSTS & SOURCES

Hazelnut flour can be used instead of almond flour. Add vanilla and spices for other flavor boosts; more variations and video how-to about this recipe on my blog. Also there, find equipment and ingredient links at: greensmoothiegourmet.com/recommendations/

Vegan Cream Cheese Frosting

Coconut milk is high in nutrition and immune-strengthening properties, including lauric acid which has been found to reduce viruses and bacteria that cause infections. With the added nutrition and lower sugar, this whipped cream makes a healthier frosting. What gives it the cream cheese bite? Apple cider vinegar, a powerful immunity booster as well.

MAKES 1 CUP

1 (13.6oz) can full fat coconut milk
5 tbsp organic powdered sugar
1 tbsp fresh lemon juice
1 tsp apple cider vinegar (ACV)

EASY
CAKES & COOKIES

Immunity & Detox

PREPARATION

1. Chill a (13.6oz) can of full fat coconut milk overnight, scoop out the solids, and set aside for this recipe. You should retrieve about 1/2 cup to 2/3 cup of solid coconut cream. Refrigerate the remaining liquid for smoothies made within the next 2 days.
2. Put your mixing bowl in the freezer for 15 minutes before mixing the frosting.
3. When you are ready to make frosting, open the can carefully and pour off the liquid. Reserve the liquid for other recipes, including smoothies.
4. To the chilled bowl, add the solids from the can and whip until you have a smooth texture. Pour in the sugar, lemon and vanilla. And whip again.
5. Put the frosting into a piping bag and pipe immediately, or dollop on to fruit or cake.
6. If frosting is too soft for piping, refrigerate for an hour or add in a thickener.

(2 tbsp) *protein 0.5 fiber 0.5 fat 4.8 calories 133 sugars 5.7 carbs 6.2*

SWAPS, BOOSTS & SOURCES

You can use lime instead of lemon juice, although the flavor will be milder and have less of a tang. For a crisper stiffness for piping, add a tsp of arrowroot, tapioca powder or cornstarch. Find current links to the ingredients and equipment I used, and nutritional studies at: greensmoothiegourmet.com/resources/

Pumpkin Candy Stars

It's the stuff of healthy candy store dreams! This mood booster is a star at helping you knock down those sugar cravings without consuming unhealthy refined sugar. High in healthy plant-based fats as well as vitamins B and E, this sweet treat actually kicks up your metabolism, wipes out your cravings, and reduces stress. And the spicy cinnamon helps keep your blood sugar levels balanced. Definitely a sweet treat to put anyone in a very good mood.

MAKES 1 1/2 CUP MIXTURE

1 cup pumpkin puree (or use sweet potato puree)
1/2 cup coconut butter (homemade or bought)
2 dates (soaked, pitted)
2 tsp cinnamon

EASY
CAKES & COOKIES

Good Mood Food
& Stress-Reducer

PREPARATION

1. If you want to make homemade coconut butter, add 1 cup shredded coconut, unsweetened, to a high-speed blender. Blend the coconut until it turns to butter, in a few minutes.
2. If you intend to use store-bought coconut butter, uncover jar and put it in a pot of boiling water. Stir and chop until it is melted, about 3-4 minutes as well.
3. In a blender, process the pumpkin puree, dates and cinnamon until smooth. Pour in the creamy coconut butter and blend until combined.
4. Pour the mixture into a frosting bag with a tip to make shaped candies. Or fill the bottom of a mini cupcake tin to make coins. Or pour mixture into molds. I have links to the heart and star molds I used on my resources page on the blog.
5. Freeze your candies until hardened. Coconut butter melts at 76 F , so you should keep them frozen until you are ready to eat them.

(1-inch candy) protein 0.5 fiber 1.2 fat 2.9 calories 35 sugars 1.1 carbs 2.6

SWAPS, BOOSTS & SOURCES

Feel free to use sweet potato puree or even butternut squash instead of pumpkin. The pumpkin puree I used is unsweetened, and from a 15 oz. organic, BPA-free can. Do not mistake this for canned pumpkin pie filling. Find current links to the ingredients and equipment I used, and nutritional studies at: greensmoothiegourmet.com/resources/

Almond Shortbread Tart

The perfect bed-time snack, with almonds and coconuts lulling the body to sleep with melatonin, tryptophan, as well as magnesium and potassium. And the coconut butter provides fiber and a feeling of fullness, so you won't be woken mid-sleep by hunger-pains. Goodnight.

MAKES 6-INCH ROUND TART

1/2 cup almond flour
3 tbsp coconut flour
2 tbsp maple syrup
3 tbsp coconut butter (homemade or store-bought)

EASY
CAKES & COOKIES

Sleep Support

PREPARATION

1. Preheat oven to 350 F. Line a 6-inch round tart pan with a sheet of round parchment paper.
2. If you want to make homemade coconut butter, add 1 cup shredded coconut, unsweetened, to a high-speed blender. Blend the coconut until it turns to butter, in a few minutes.
3. If you intend to use store-bought coconut butter, uncover jar and put it in a pot of boiling water. Stir and chop until it is melted, about 3-4 minutes as well.
4. In a large bowl, stir together the flours, syrup and melted butter. Form a dough and press it into the tart pan. Poke holes in the dough to prevent air bubbles from forming in the oven.
5. Bake for 10 minutes or until edges turn a golden color. Cool and enjoy as is or drizzle on more melted coconut butter and almond slices.

(1/6th of tart) protein 4 fiber 6 fat 14.2 calories 196 sugars 5.4 carbs 14

SWAPS, BOOSTS & SOURCES

If you have them, you can add cherries which are a strong source of sleep-inducing melatonin. Walnuts are also high in melatonin, and pumpkin seeds are high in magnesium, also important to sleep. Find current links to the ingredients and equipment I used, and nutritional studies at: greensmoothiegourmet.com/resources/

Sunflower Fudge Cups

Sunflower seed butter and coconut butter are both easy to make, highly nutritious and powerful metabolism-boosters. Thus, both butters are magical members of the weight-control club, with not only the ability to speed up the metabolism, but also the ability to suppress the appetite and provide impressive nutrients including E and B vitamins, niacin, and folates. If you don't need nut-free, use creamy homemade pecan butter instead of sunflower butter, see my how-to below.

MAKES 18 MINI CUPS OR 6 CUPS

1/2 cup sunflower seed butter
1/2 cup coconut butter (homemade or store-bought)
1 1/2 cup dark chocolate chips or bar
3 tbsp cinnamon

EASY
CAKES & COOKIES

Weight Control & Workout Food

PREPARATION

1. Prepare coconut butter. If you want to make homemade coconut butter, add 2 cups shredded coconut, unsweetened, to a high-speed blender. Blend the coconut until it turns to butter, in a few minutes. This will create about 1 cup butter; store the rest in jar.
2. If you intend to use store-bought coconut butter, uncover jar and put it in a pot of boiling water. Stir and chop until it is melted, about 3-4 minutes as well.
3. Melt the chocolate in a heat-resistant glass measuring cup in a microwave for 60 seconds. Stir in sunflower butter (I used store-bought) and cinnamon, then stir until all is melted and incorporated.
4. Line a mini-cupcake pan with 18 liners or a cupcake tin with 6.
5. Pour in melted chocolate, filling each cup 1/4, chill for 10 minutes. Then add coconut butter, again fill each cup 1/4, chill for 10 minutes, and then add last layer of chocolate. Chill until set, dust with cacao powder. Store refrigerated.

protein 3.4 fiber 3.3 fat 15.6 calories 202 sugars 8.1 carbs 14.3

SWAPS, BOOSTS & SOURCES

To use pecan butter instead of sunflower butter, toast raw pecans in a skillet, and blend the cooled nuts into pecan butter, adding spices to taste. Find current links to the ingredients and equipment I used, and nutritional studies at: greensmoothiegourmet.com/resources/

Samoa Coconut Cookies

This healthy copycat of the traditional Girl Scout favorite is full of fiber, iron and potassium, supporting hair, skin, nails and providing you energy and stamina. One exceptionally healthy ingredient is coconut which provides the authentic flavor so inherent in the traditional recipe.

MAKES 10 COOKIES

1 cup date paste (8-10 dates, soaked & pitted + 1/2 cup water)
1/4 cup coconut flour
1/4 cup shredded coconut, unsweetened
3/4 cup dark chocolate chips or bar

EASY
CAKES & COOKIES

Hair, Skin &
Nail Support

PREPARATION

1. Soak the dates overnight or in boiling water; remove pits. Blend dates into a smooth paste.
2. Line a quarter cookie sheet with parchment paper. Spread shredded coconut and toast at 400 F for 5 minutes. Set the shredded coconut into a large mixing bowl, and re-line the cookie sheet.
3. To a bowl, next add the date paste, and flour. Hand-mix until a batter is formed. Depending on the size and moisture in your dates, you may have to add a bit more flour or water until dough is formable, but not sticking to your fingers.
4. Freeze the dough for 30 minutes. Make perfect circles by pressing 1 tbsp of chilled dough into a 2-inch round cookie cutter. Poke out a center hole.
5. Set the pan in the freezer for one hour.
6. After one hour, melt chocolate in bowl in microwave in 60-second intervals.
7. Remove frozen circles and dip only bottom in melted chocolate, holding the cookies until the chocolate is set, then set it upside down on a cooling rack.
8. Once all cookie bottoms are coated and hardened, set them bottom down on a cookie sheet, lined with parchment paper. Drizzle with chocolate. Keep cookies refrigerated.

protein 0.8 fiber 0.9 fat 2.6 calories 61 sugars 8.4 carbs 10.6

SWAPS, BOOSTS & SOURCES

Flour substitutions are not recommended as coconut flour is unusually absorbent. Find current links to the ingredients and equipment I used, and nutritional studies at: greens-moothiegourmet.com/resources/

Chocolate Mousse Lollipops

Controlling inflammation we now know is the key to successfully thwarting disease and staying healthy. Avocado, the main ingredient in this mousse, has a strong anti-inflammatory potential, with a high ORAC, the ability to devour body-damaging free radicals. Combined with antioxidant-rich dark chocolate chips, and you have a delightfully healthy fun treat.

MAKES 1 CUP MOUSSE

1 large avocado, peeled

1 1/4 cup dark chocolate chips

1/8 cup milk (I used hemp milk)

1-2 tbsp maple syrup

EASY
CAKES & COOKIES

Anti-Inflammatory

PREPARATION

1. Melt the dark chocolate in a 2-cup measuring cup by putting it in microwave for 60 seconds and stirring until all chips are melted.
2. Add 1/4 of the melted chocolate to a food processor or blender. Next add the avocado, milk and 1 tbsp maple syrup. Blend until smooth, taste-test and decide if the additional maple syrup is needed.
3. Spoon mousse into silicon lollipop molds, and tap the mold to even the surface. Insert sticks. Typical lollipop molds hold about 8 lollipops per tray. Refrigerate any leftover mousse to serve within 2 days as a healthy pudding.
4. Freeze the lollipops four hours. Re-melt the 1 cup of chocolate and let chocolate stand to cool but not solidify - about 10 minutes.
5. Remove frozen lollipops from the mold, and dip each in melted chocolate. Hold each lollipop dripping off over the chocolate until it is fairly solid, a few minutes each. It is tedious. Set the coated lollipop on a cooling rack.
6. If you want to pipe the tell-tale swirls, use your favorite white frosting and a writing tip.. Store the pops in the freezer.

protein 2.4 fiber 3.7 fat 14.7 calories 224 sugars 15.5 carbs 21.5

SWAPS, BOOSTS & SOURCES

Swap the avocado for 1/2 cup coconut cream - solid portion of a chilled can of full-fat coconut milk - for a similar texture. Find current links to the ingredients and equipment I used, and nutritional studies at: greensmoothiegourmet.com/resources/

Nutritious Sides & Snacks

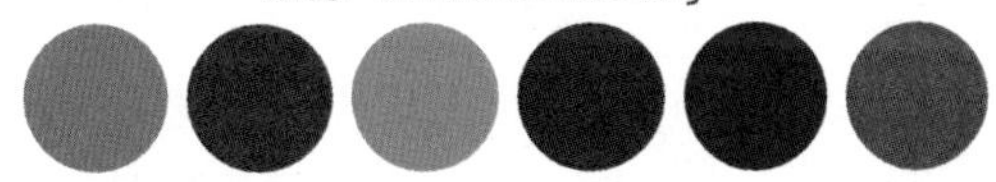

Chickpea Crumb Cauliflower

Cauliflower is rapidly becoming mainstream as a valuable source of protein and fiber. Add in protein-rich chickpea crumbs, with aquafaba used as a binder instead of eggs, and this side is an awesomely healthy addition to your day. Make homemade chickpea crumbs by dry roasting chickpeas on a cookie sheet, and grinding in a food processor. Of course you can coat cauliflower florets in traditional breadcrumbs, but why miss the additional protein?

MAKES 12 BITES

1 cauliflower head, cut into florets (about 4 cups)
1 cup chickpea crumbs (or breadcrumbs)
1/2 cup aquafaba (liquid from chickpea can)
3 tbsp fresh herbs (basil, oregano, rosemary)

NUTRITIOUS
SIDES & SNACKS

Protein & Fiber

PREPARATION

1. Preheat your oven to 425 F. Line a cookie sheet with parchment paper.
2. To make chickpea crumbs, open a can of organic garbanzo beans/chickpeas, reserve the liquid, rinse the beans, and spread the beans over parchment paper. Bake the chickpeas for 30 minutes, shake the pan a bit to loosen and overturn the beans, then bake another 30 minutes. Allow them to cool completely and grind to a crumb in a food processor or a high-powered blender.
3. To prepare the cauliflower bites, line another cookie sheet with parchment paper and set out two mixing bowls. In one, put 9 tbsp of aquafaba (liquid from chickpea can).
In the other bowl, pour in the chickpea crumbs, and stir in dried seasonings.
4. Dip each cauliflower floret first in the aquafaba, and then in the chickpea crumbs, and lay on the parchment-lined cookie sheet. Bake for 30 minutes or until golden brown. Serve with your favorite sauce.

protein 4.2 fiber 1.2 fat 1.6 calories 60 sugars 1.4 carbs 8.3

SWAPS, BOOSTS & SOURCES

You can use flax seed eggs as a binder instead of aquafaba, and swap out your favorite spices. Chickpea crumbs can be bought. Find current links to the ingredients and equipment I used, and nutritional studies at: greensmoothiegourmet.com/resources/

Quinoa Herb Flatbread

A 4-ingredient bread. Take quinoa, and a few other ingredients, make a few passes with your magic wand, and you have bread. And not just any bread. A plant-based bread high in magnesium, which relaxes blood vessels, producing fewer headaches. Also, a bread that provides a complete protein - all nine essential amino acids - a rarity in the plant kingdom.

18 (2X3-INCH) SLICES

1 cup quinoa (raw & rinsed)

1/2 cup cashew milk (or your favorite)

1 tsp baking powder

Spices (1 tsp onion powder, 1 tsp Italian seasoning)

NUTRITIOUS SIDES & SNACKS

Energizer & Brain Support

PREPARATION

1. Put the quinoa in a strainer and rinse thoroughly under running water to remove the outside bitter coating.
2. Preheat the oven to 425 F. Line a 13x9-inch cookie sheet with parchment paper. Have another same-size sheet of parchment ready to help flip the bread during baking.
3. Blend the rinsed quinoa, milk, baking powder and spices in a high-speed blender. Blend for several minutes, stopping to scrap down sides. A high-speed blender is necessary to reach a smooth consistency. Quinoa can vary in absorbancy so be sure to add a bit more milk if you don't have a pancake batter consistency.
4. Using a spatula, spread the batter in pan, not reaching edges so it doesn't stick to them.
5. Bake for 15 minutes or until golden. Remove from oven, and quickly lay second parchment on top, and without burning your fingers, flip over the pan so bread is upside down on new parchment. Lift new parchment and bread dough back on the pan, and bake that side for at least 5 minutes or until slightly golden.
6. Cut bread into rectangles using a pizza cutter or knife.
7. For grill marks and a crispy texture, press each rectangle in a panini press.

protein 1.4 fiber 0.7 fat 0.6 calories 37 sugars 0.2 carbs 6.4

SWAPS, BOOSTS & SOURCES

Vary the ground spices to your taste. Optionally, sprinkle toppings to raw batter, such as flax, chia, sunflower, pumpkin, and hemp. Find current links to the ingredients and equipment I used, and nutritional studies at: greensmoothiegourmet.com/resources/

Spicy Carrot Latkes

Vegetables are great detoxers, but carrots are especially powerful, packed with vitamin A, which removes toxins and is antiseptic to the body. Add to that fresh spices which stimulate the body's main detoxification processes. Baking them this way, as crunchy spicy hand cakes, is oil-free, thus healthier and convenient. Eat them as is, sandwiched with leafy greens, or crumbled into a salad.

MAKES 12 LATKES

2 cups carrots, either shredded or spiralized

6 flax seed eggs

1/2 cup chickpea flour (or almond or oat flour)

Spices, 4 tsp each (onion powder, tarragon, rosemary, dill)

PREPARATION

1. Preheat oven to 350 F. Line a cookie sheet with parchment paper.
2. Prepare the seed eggs. Stir 2 tbsp of ground flax seeds into 6 tbsp of water. Set aside for 10 minutes.
3. Prepare the carrots by either chopping or shredding or spiralizing to create curly strings.
4. Chop the herbs finely. Use ground spices if you don't have access to all fresh.
5. In a large bowl, combine all four ingredients. Mix by hand and form thin patties about 3 inches in diameter. Line them on the pan, brushing top with olive oil.
6. Bake for 25 minutes or until latkes are dry and crusty. Flip, and cook for 2 minutes on other side.
7. Serve as is or with your favorite dip, in a sandwich, or crumbled in a salad.

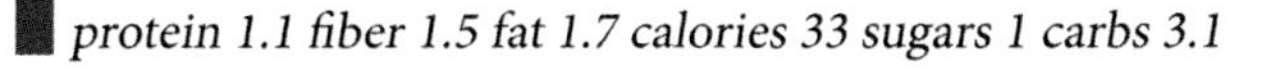
protein 1.1 fiber 1.5 fat 1.7 calories 33 sugars 1 carbs 3.1

SWAPS, BOOSTS & SOURCES

Swap other protein flours for the chickpea flour, including oat or lentil. Consider adding chopped kale, eggplant or zucchini. Find current links to the ingredients and equipment I used, and nutritional studies at: greensmoothiegourmet.com/resources/

Mini Zucchini Pizzas

Zucchini is loaded with B6, riboflavin, folate, and vitamin C, all nutrients instrumental in boosting spirits. Add in tomato sauce, loaded with stress-reducing antioxidants, and mushrooms high vitamin D, and we have a snack that truly calms. Plus, it's delicious, and easy to make. I added tomato sauce, mushrooms and dairy-free cheese to top mine, but you can see the potential for further customization.

MAKES 12-18 PIZZAS

1-2 large zucchini, sliced
1/2 cup mushrooms, diced
3/4 cup marinara sauce
3/4 cup dairy-free cheese

NUTRITIOUS
SIDES & SNACKS

Good Mood Food
& Stress-Reducer

PREPARATION

1. Preheat oven to 500 F (broil). Line a cookie sheet with foil. Rub foil lightly with olive oil.
2. Wash zucchini, and slice uniformly, at least 1/4-inch in width, and set them in a colander that is in a bowl. Toss the slices in a bit of salt, and set it aside for 30 minutes.
3. Drain the zucchini slices, discard the water. Now the zucchini should be less soggy. Skip this step if you don't want the extra salted flavor in the zucchini slices.
4. Heat a skillet with 1-2 tbsp of olive oil. Brown each zucchini disc about 3 minutes on each side, until a brown crust forms on each side.
5. Place the zucchini discs in rows on the cookie sheet. Top with mushrooms, marinara and shredded cheese. I used dairy-free
6. Place the cookie sheet in the broiler for 1 minute or until the cheese is melted. Sprinkle with parsley and serve.
7. These are best eaten fresh and hot, although can be refrigerated and re-heated.

protein 0.5 fiber 0.5 fat 0.1 calories 8 sugars 1.3 carbs 1.7

SWAPS, BOOSTS & SOURCES

You can swap the zucchini for butternut squash or eggplant. Additional toppings for these pizzas are endless. Find current links to the ingredients and equipment I used, and nutritional studies at: greensmoothiegourmet.com/resources/

White Bean Meatballs

Perfect comfort food meal that happens to help you get a good night's sleep. White beans are packed with protein, fiber and vitamin Bs, all of which help regulate your sleep wake cycles. The protein flour before bed provides you with a bit of tryptophan, an amino acid that can help promote sleep. Mix in spices, slather these meatballs with ketchup, and serve up on a sub loaf.

MAKES 6 MEATBALLS

1 (15oz can) white beans (organic, BPA-free)
1/4 cup flour (almond or chickpea)
1/2 cup ketchup, refined-sugar-free
1 tsp each (onion powder, garlic powder, basil, oregano, nutritional yeast)

PREPARATION

1. Preheat the oven to 400 F. Line a quarter cookie sheet with foil, brush foil lightly with olive oil.
2. Drain and rinse the beans, and add them to a mixing bowl with flour, 1/4 cup ketchup and ground herbs and spices.
3. Use a spoon or your hands to blend the ingredients. Adjust texture so the mixture can be molded into meatball-shape: add flour if it is too wet, add ketchup if it is too dry.
4. Next, taste-test and adjust seasonings. Typically I add more basil and oregano and nutritional yeast, and sometimes a pinch of pepper.
5. Fill a bowl with remaining 1/4 cup ketchup, and dip your hands into the ketchup and generously coat your hands. Using ketchup-covered hands, roll mixture into 6 meatballs, and set them on the pan.
6. Bake them uncovered for 10 minutes, then use a spoon to nudge them, releasing them from the foil. Bake them another 10 minutes, then flip them carefully and bake the other side another 10 minutes. Coat them in your favorite marinara sauce and eat alone, or on pasta, or in a sandwich with your favorite toppings.

protein 3.2 fiber 4.1 fat 2 calories 88 sugars 5.5 carbs 15.7

SWAPS, BOOSTS & SOURCES

If you want a sturdier meatball, swap the flour for rolled oats. Boost by adding chopped green onions, parsley, even diced mushrooms. Find current links to the ingredients and equipment I used, and nutritional studies at: greensmoothiegourmet.com/resources/

Mexican Pozole Ramen

Pozole is a soup made with hominy that has traditions in the Mexican culture. Its backbone is hominy, a type of corn made healthier and easier to digest. Hominy, it seems, has earned the respect of those looking to control weight. Rich in carbohydrates and low in fats, it is satiating but low calorie. And it's perfect in a workout meal as it provides a boost in energy-producing vitamin Bs. A comforting, filling, interesting soup, easy on the waistline.

MAKES 3 CUPS SOUP

2 cups organic vegetable broth
1 (15oz) can of organic hominy
2 cups ramen noodles
Spices, 1 tsp each (onion powder, garlic, cilantro, oregano)

PREPARATION

1. Heat the broth, stirring in the spices.
2. Add in the hominy, and simmer 20 minutes. Add in the ramen noodles after hominy has simmered for 15 minutes.
3. Serve topped with celery, avocado, and red bell pepper.
4. If you want to use fresh (dry) hominy kernels instead of canned. First rinse 2 cups of dried hominy kernels (looks like corn), submerge into a fresh pot of water, and let sit at room temperature overnight.
5. The next day, drain, put the hominy kernals in a fresh pot of water, and simmer low for up to 2 hours or until soft. Use 15oz of this in place of the can of hominy in the recipe.

protein 4 fiber 1.4 fat 1.4 calories 65 sugars 1.5 carbs 8.5

SWAPS, BOOSTS & SOURCES

The addition of lime brightens this soup's flavor. This recipe can be used as a base, and thus add as many fresh veggies as you want, including broccoli, cauliflower, carrots, and more. Find current links to the ingredients and equipment I used, and nutritional studies at: greensmoothiegourmet.com/resources/

Baked Protein Asparagus

Asparagus contains large amounts of the beauty vitamins, A, C and E, each of which enriches healthy growth of hair, skin and nails. Add to this the delicious nutrition from protein-rich almond crumbs and flax seed, and you have an extremely nutritious snack. Instead of traditional egg as a binder, flax seed eggs are used to help the crumb stick.

MAKES 12

12 asparagus stalks

1/2 cup almond crumbs (or chickpea crumbs)

3/4 cup flax seed eggs (6 tbsp flax seed + 1/2 cup water)

Spices, 1 tsp each (garlic powder, basil, oregano)

NUTRITIOUS
SIDES & SNACKS

Hair, Skin &
Nail Support

PREPARATION

1. Preheat oven to 425 F. Line a cookie sheet with parchment paper.
2. In a shallow bowl the length of asparagus, make the flax seed eggs by stirring 6 tbsp flax seed into 1/2 cup of water. Set aside for 10 minutes to allow it to gel.
3. To make almond crumbs, roughly process 1/2 cup of almonds in a food processor into crumbs. Not too long or it will become butter. Stale almonds work best; or roast your almonds for 10 minutes at 425 F, and allow to cool before processing into crumbs. Pour the crumbs in a bowl, and stir in spices.
4. Wash the asparagus, trim and discard an inch or so of the white fibrous bottoms.
5. Arrange bowls in a row, first the flax seed mixture, next the almond crumbs, and last, the cookie sheet.
6. Dip each spear into the flax egg mixture, and then the crumbs, rolling until the spear is coated. Repeat if necessary, for a heavier coating. Then line them up on the pan.
7. Bake at 425 F for 20 minutes. Spray with olive oil if you would like. Serve with refined-sugar-free ketchup. These are best eaten fresh and hot, although can be refrigerated and re-heated.

protein 4.7 fiber 0.9 fat 0.5 calories 33 sugars 0.5 carbs 3.2

SWAPS, BOOSTS & SOURCES

Make nut-free by swapping the almond crumbs for chickpea crumbs - find my homemade recipe on Chickpea Crumb Cauliflower recipe in this book, or they can be store-bought. Find current links to the ingredients and equipment I used, and nutritional studies at: greensmoothiegourmet.com/resources/

One Pot Spinach Pasta

One pot pasta is genius. You boil everything, even the pasta, in one go! And it's well-known that foods that fight inflammation are useful in both losing weight and fighting off illness. But some foods that are especially powerful inflammation-fighters are overlooked. One such food is oregano, with an ORAC (ability to devour damaging free radicals) value of nearly 14,000.

MAKES 2 CUPS

1 cup chopped spinach

2 cups chopped tomatoes

1 cup chopped yellow onion

1 cup fresh herbs, combined (oregano, basil, 2 garlic cloves)

PREPARATION

1. Chop spinach, onions, tomatoes and herbs and put in a cast iron skillet.
2. Sprinkle with olive oil, and add 12 ounces of your favorite pasta and 3 cups of water.
3. Set on the stove and bring to a boil, stirring constantly. Let it simmer for about 7 minutes, stirring until pasta is cooked and water is evaporated.
4. Serve with sprinklings of nutritional yeast and olives.
5. Store refrigerated for 3 days.

protein 1.9 fiber 2.6 fat 0.3 calories 43 sugars 4.9 carbs 9.4

SWAPS, BOOSTS & SOURCES

You might want to add mushrooms to this dish. Find current links to the ingredients and equipment I used, and nutritional studies at: greensmoothiegourmet.com/resources/

Healthy Pops & Ice Cream

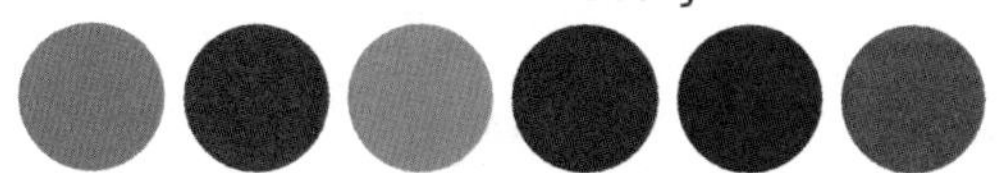

Mango Almond Yogurt Popsicles

Mangos and almonds are an unusual yet surprisingly healthy combination, presenting a dessert high in protein and fiber, as well as other essential nutrients. The mango's texture lends itself perfectly to a frosted popsicle state. Add in creamy homemade almond yogurt to smooth out the iciness and add a slice of lemon to each pop for a tangy surprise.

MAKES 10 POPSICLES

1 1/2 cups mango
1/2 cup yogurt (homemade or bought)
1/4 cup lemon juice from two lemons
Zest, slices off one lemon

HEALTHY POPS
& ICE CREAM

Protein & Fiber

PREPARATION

1. If you are using homemade yogurt, begin making it roughly one day ahead. To make almond yogurt, which is what I used here, soak 1 cup almonds in water in refrigerator overnight. The next day, rinse the almonds, and blend with 1 1/3 cup water, 2 tbsp lemon juice and the powder from 1 probiotic supplement capsules. Pour mixture into a measuring cup, cover with a cloth held by elastic band. Place in dark corner on kitchen counter for 12 hours. After that, stir it up, and your yogurt is ready to eat and use in this recipe. Refrigerated and covered, it will keep for three days.
2. To proceed with making popsicles, prepare the lemons. Remove the zest off one, and slice. Squeeze the juice out of two others. Two lemons should provide 1/4 cup of juice.
3. Blend up the yogurt, juice, zest, and mango in a high-speed blender.
4. Insert one thin lemon slice into each popsicle opening, pressing to one side. Pour the mixture into a popsicle mold.
5. Freeze popsicle 30 minutes, insert sticks and freeze an additional four hours. Store covered in freezer.

protein 1 fiber 0.4 fat 0.3 calories 25 sugars 4.4 carbs 4.7

SWAPS, BOOSTS & SOURCES

Yogurt made like this can be thin; make it thicker by adding 1 teaspoon of white chia seeds before the 12-hour wait and blend after that to break down the seeds. Find my recommend popsicle mold, other equipment and ingredients I used, as well as nutritional studies at: greensmoothiegourmet.com/resources/

Raspberry Lemon Granita

Raspberries, as do most berries, have a high concentration of antioxidants that flock to the brain, supporting thinking processes, memory and improving communication abilities. Making them into this recipe is a bit high maintenance at first, but you'll be left with a healthy treat whose unusual texture is actually retained over several days so you can spoon it into a bowl as you wish. In southern Italy, it's eaten for breakfast with brioche.

MAKES 12 SERVINGS

4 cups raspberries, frozen
1 1/2 cups water
1/4 cup lemon juice
2 tbsp maple syrup

HEALTHY POPS
& ICE CREAM

Energizer &
Brain Support

PREPARATION

1. Blend the water, thawed raspberries, lemon juice and syrup. Taste-test the mixture for enough sweetness, adding one more tablespoon syrup if you want it sweeter.
2. Pour the mixture into a 13x9-inch pan baking dish.
3. Place covered in freezer.
4. Every 45 minutes, stir and scrap the semi-frozen mixture with a fork or edge of spoon. At first you will be stirring a slurry. After a few more times, it will begin to harden more and you will be scrapping off crystals as deep as you can. Your eventual goal is to have a container full of ice crystals or granita. This takes about 2-3 hours.
5. Once you have your granita finalized. Keep stored covered in freezer. Serve in ice cream bowls with mint leaves.

protein 0.5 fiber 2.7 fat 0.3 calories 31sugars 3.9 carbs 7.2

SWAPS, BOOSTS & SOURCES

The variations are many. Use any berry, and try adding herbs, such as basil with watermelon, tarragon with strawberries, mint with blueberries. Find current links to the ingredients and equipment I used, and nutritional studies at: greensmoothiegourmet.com/resources/

Miso Ginger Ice Cream

Did you know we have five basic tastes, not four? Sweet, bitter, salty, sour, and "umami" is the fifth. The word is Japanese for "a pleasant savory taste". Really? A savory ice cream. Yes! The flavor here is a mix of sweet and salt with a gingery bite. And healthy! Raw miso, a salty fermented paste, provides beneficial bacteria conducive with good health. A sophisticated treat that is as nutritional as it is unusual.

MAKES 2 CUPS

1 (13.6oz) can full fat coconut milk
1/3 cup maple syrup
1-inch fresh ginger
2 tbsp miso paste (any color)

HEALTHY POPS
& ICE CREAM

Immunity & Detox

PREPARATION

1. Chill the can of coconut milk - not to separate liquids and solids, just to chill. Shake the can vigorously before use in this recipe.
2. If you are using an ice cream maker, you need to freeze the ice cream maker bowl overnight. Check your ice cream maker's directions.
3. Prepare your ginger by peeling off skin as you would peel a potato, slice and chop, and crush pieces in a garlic-press. Capture all juice and pulp in a small bowl and set aside.
4. Into a blender, pour entire contents of both cans of milk, syrup, ginger, and paste. Blend until smooth. If your mixture seems curdled at this step or speckly, keep blending until milky and not separated, about 2-3 minutes. If that doesn't remove specks, heat it on the stove, stirring until creamy, then let mixture cool to room temperature.
5. Set the room temperature mixture in refrigerator to chill for 1 hour prior to adding to ice cream maker. If you intend to use an ice cream maker, following machine's directions.
6. If you want to make the ice cream without a maker, pour this mixture into a glass pan, place in freezer and stir every 45 minutes until you reach desired consistency. This might take several hours to reach a scoopable texture. Sprinkle with fresh ginger to serve.

(1/2 cup) protein 3.2 fiber 2.6 fat 22.1 calories 297 sugars 19.2 carbs 25.8

SWAPS, BOOSTS & SOURCES

Swap maple syrup for organic cane sugar for a whiter color. Or use monk syrup to make keto. Find miso paste in refrigeration section, near tofu. Find current links to the ingredients and equipment I used, and nutritional studies at: greensmoothiegourmet.com/resources/

250ml

Chocolate Macadamia Butter

Macadamia nuts are a strong stress-reducer and have the same healthy heart omega-9 found in olive oil. The creamy white nut is also high in fiber, iron and protein, and essential minerals the body can't produce. Here they are soaked and blended with avocado, which holds healthy fats and all essential amino acids, and raw cacao powder, a huge mood-booster, rich in magnesium and other happy powers.

MAKES 1 CUP

2 cups macadamia nuts
2 tbsp cacao powder
1/2 avocado, ripe and soft
2-4 tbsp maple syrup

HEALTHY POPS
& ICE CREAM

Good Mood Food
& Stress-Reducer

PREPARATION

1. Unlike with cashew nuts, you do not soak your macadamia nuts before making nut butter, their oils are too delicate. For that reason, it is important to buy them fresh.
2. In a high-speed blender, blend up the macadamia nuts as smooth as possible.
3. Add in the cacao powder and avocado. If you want a non-sweet chocolate butter, leave off the maple syrup. If you choose to sweeten the butter, at this point, taste test and add the maple syrup a tablespoon at a time, processing and tasting in between, stopping when it is sweet enough for you.
4. Keep in a covered container, refrigerated, for one week.

(1 tbsp) protein 1.9 fiber 2.6 fat 14.4 calories 152 sugars 3.8 carbs 7.5

SWAPS, BOOSTS & SOURCES

Macadamia nuts are expensive so you can substitute half for cashews. Find current links to the ingredients and equipment I used, and nutritional studies at: greensmoothiegourmet.com/resources/

Cherry-Mango Dole Whip

This refreshing treat is modeled after the trendy frozen soft serve available at Disney parks. The original Disney version is pineapple in flavor. My version uses cherries, high in sleep-supporting melatonin, and mango, which increases the body's iron absorption. Both ingredients are so important to sleep. The addition of protein-rich navy beans and coconut cream, support sustained sleep, preventing disturbances due to hunger.

MAKES 2 CUPS

1 cup frozen cherries

1 cup frozen mango

1 (13.6oz) can full fat coconut milk

1/4 cup white beans (navy, rinsed)

HEALTHY POPS & ICE CREAM

Sleep Support

PREPARATION

1. Chill a (13.6oz) can of full fat coconut milk overnight, scoop out the solids, and set aside for this recipe. You should have about 1/2 cup. Refrigerate the remaining liquid for smoothies made within the next 2 days.
2. To a blender, add the cherries and mango and blend until you have a smooth puree.
3. To that mixture, add the coconut cream and white beans.
4. Blend until creamy, about 30 seconds in a high-speed blender.
5. Pour the mixture into a piping bag and pipe into swirls in small glasses. Or just spoon it and eat.
6. To store, spoon mixture into a freezer-friendly container or a parchment-lined loaf pan, and freeze.

(1/2 cup) protein 4.5 fiber 4 fat 7.6 calories 158 sugars 11.7 carbs 21

SWAPS, BOOSTS & SOURCES

Swap cherries for pineapple to make the treat more like the tropical dessert found at Disney parks. White beans can be left out; texture will be thinner. Find current links to the ingredients and equipment I used, and nutritional studies at: greensmoothiegourmet.com/resources/

Classic Vanilla Banana Ice Cream

Bananas are high in potassium and fiber, as well as various essential vitamins, including vitamin C. They are often used in healthy recipes, to thicken smoothies, and as a natural ice cream base, largely because magically once frozen and blended, you have a neutral-flavored ice cream that rivals dairy in texture and nutrition. The perfect energizing and appetite-controlling treat.

MAKES 2 CUPS

4 cups bananas (ripe, chopped, frozen)
2 tbsp almond milk (or your choice)
1 tsp vanilla
pinch of salt

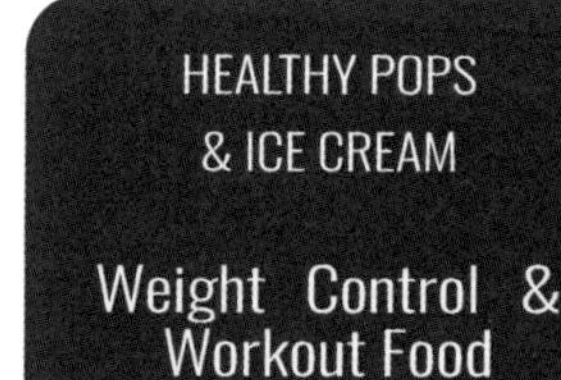

HEALTHY POPS
& ICE CREAM
Weight Control &
Workout Food

PREPARATION

1. Prepare bananas the night before. Ripe but not bruised bananas work best. Peel the bananas, chop into 1-inch chunks, and freeze on a cookie sheet so they don't freeze together in a chunk.
2. The next day, line a 8x4-inch loaf pan with parchment paper.
3. Measure out 4 cups of banana chunks and add them to a high-speed blender. You can wait 10-minutes or so to let them thaw a bit to save your blender blades.
4. When ready, process until bananas are creamy. Add in the milk or more if needed to help process. Add in vanilla and salt.
5. Pour this mixture into the loaf pan and freeze for about 30 minutes, and then scoop. Longer if you want the ice cream to be firmer. We packed ours between chocolate chip cookies, and re-froze to make ice cream sandwiches.

(1/2 cup) protein 2.1 fiber 3.9 fat 1.8 calories 164 sugars 21.4 carbs 38.3

SWAPS, BOOSTS & SOURCES

Ice cream can be made with coconut cream if you don't like bananas. See Miso Ginger Ice Cream recipe in this book. Feel free to customize, adding chocolate chips, nuts, chunks for fruit. Find current links to the ingredients and equipment I used, and nutritional studies at: greensmoothiegourmet.com/resources/

Matcha Beauty Popsicles

Matcha green tea powder is packed with antioxidants, specifically polyphenols, that are powerful anti-agers, and even boost metabolism. Matcha is the power-version of green tea. Green tea is made from steeping dried green tea leaves whereas Matcha powder is super quality green tea leaves ground up into powder. You are drinking the actual tea leaves; not just liquid steeped in leaves. Therein lies the power.

MAKES 6 POPSICLES

3 cups yogurt
1/2 cup milk
1 tbsp matcha powder (ceremonial grade)
2 tbsp maple syrup

HEALTHY POPS & ICE CREAM

Hair, Skin & Nail Support

PREPARATION

1. Set the yogurt into a bowl, and whisk in the milk and maple syrup.
2. Put 1 cup of that mixture into a different container and stir in the matcha powder. Do not blend or the delicate powder will be damaged.
3. Taste-test the matcha mixture and add more of maple syrup if needed to offset any bitter taste. Spoon the matcha mixture into each popsicle mold. Follow with the rest of the yogurt mixture.
4. Freeze the mold for 30 minutes, and then insert the popsicle sticks. Freeze again for at least 4 hours.
5. To remove the finished pops, sit the mold into a large pot of hot water for a few seconds, and yank at the popsicle sticks to pull them out. Keep doing this until all popsicles are released. Set them on a parchment-lined cookie sheet and sprinkle with sprinkles.
6. Store in the freezer in a covered container.

protein 7.1 fiber 0.2 fat 1.7 calories 113 sugars 13.3 carbs 14.4

SWAPS, BOOSTS & SOURCES

Be sure to use ceremonial grade matcha, not cooking grade which will taste too bitter. Find current links to the ingredients and equipment I used, and nutritional studies at: greens-moothiegourmet.com/resources/

Blueberry Clove Nicecream

Yes, cloves are often found in winter holiday treats, but the spice is actually a powerful anti-inflammatory, useful in treating sore throats and other issues. So why not put it in ice cream. Blueberries are known antioxidants and, of course, bananas make a very creamy, healthy ice cream.

MAKES 2 CUPS

3 cups bananas (ripe, chopped, frozen)
1 cup blueberries, frozen
2 tbsp nut milk
1 tsp cloves

PREPARATION

1. Prepare bananas the night before. Ripe but not bruised bananas work best. Peel the bananas, chop into 1-inch chunks, and freeze on a cookie sheet so they don't freeze together in a chunk.
2. The next day, line a 8x4-inch loaf pan with parchment paper.
3. Measure out 3 cups of banana chunks and add them to a high-speed blender. Add in the blueberries, milk and cloves. You can wait 10-minutes or so for frozens to thaw a bit to save your blender blades.
4. When ready, process until texture is creamy. Add in the 2 tbsp milk or more if needed to help process. Taste-test to see if you need to add more cloves for more pronounced flavor.
5. Pour this mixture into the loaf pan and freeze for about 30 minutes, and then scoop. Longer if you want the ice cream to be firmer.

(1/2 cup) protein 1.7 fiber 4 fat 2.3 calories 138 sugars 17.6 carbs 31.4

SWAPS, BOOSTS & SOURCES

Replace the bananas with 2 cups of acai pulp, found in the freezer section of stores. Acai provides additional anti-inflammatory power as well as more fiber and other nutrients. Taste-test and add maple syrup to sweeten if needed. Find current links to the ingredients and equipment I used, and nutritional studies at: greensmoothiegourmet.com/resources/

Nourishing Hydrating Drinks

Pink Beet Smoothie Cubes

A useful make-ahead meal prep for smoothies is to make a smoothie and freeze it in ice cube trays. Then, the night before, drop 4-6 cubes in a glass, set it in the refrigerator, and blend in the morning. Use these thawed smoothie cubes as a base, adding ingredients on blending day that are customized to your needs, such as zucchini, rolled oats, seeds, avocado, spices and more.

MAKES 2 CUPS

1 cup yogurt
1 beet (peeled, chopped, raw)
1 cup coconut water
1 orange, peeled

NOURISHING
HYDRATING DRINKS

Protein & Fiber

PREPARATION

1. Scrub and chop the beet. You can also use ready-made cooked beets, or even steam your own. Just don't used jarred pickled beets.
2. Peel the orange, and add all ingredients to a high speed blender.
3. Blend up and pour into your ice cube tray. The round gummy ball tray I used here holds about 1 cup of mixture.
4. Freeze overnight, transfer the cubes into a sealed container for long-term storage.
5. To make a smoothie, transfer 4-6 cubes into a glass and refrigerate overnight. The next day, pour the melted cubes into a blender, add 1/2 cup of milk, other ingredients you choose and drink.

(1/2 cup) protein 4.8 fiber 2.3 fat 1 calories 88 sugars 12.2 carbs 14.4

SWAPS, BOOSTS & SOURCES

Swap out the raw beet for 1/2 cup of frozen pink pitaya or acai pulp, found in your grocer freezer section. Or 1/2 cup pomegranate juice, high in fiber, low in calories. Find my equipment, ingredients, and nutritional studies at: greensmoothiegourmet.com/resources/

Chocolate Hummus Shake

Hummus is the perfect healthy party dip, but it can make a delicious protein shake as well. Just blend up chickpeas, tahini, and frozen milk. Not familiar with tahini? It's a sesame seed paste, a brain booster and hormone-balancer. Find quality tahini in the quality nut butter aisle. This shake is rich in protein and iron, and a strong energizer.

MAKES 3 SHAKES

1/2 (15oz can) garbanzo beans/chickpeas (organic, BPA-free)
1/4 cup tahini (unsweetened sesame seed butter)
1/4 cup chocolate chips, melted
1 1/2 cup almond milk

NOURISHING HYDRATING DRINKS

Energizer & Brain Support

PREPARATION

1. Melt the chocolate chips in a heat-safe measuring cup in a microwave at 60 seconds.
2. Add the melted chocolate, beans, tahini and almond milk to a blender and process until smooth.
3. Chill the smoothie before drinking, or freeze half the almond milk into cubes before blending.

protein 10.9 fiber 9.9 fat 20.5 calories 372 sugars 14.2 carbs 38.4

SWAPS, BOOSTS & SOURCES

Would you like it sweeter? Add 2 tbsp of maple syrup. For a deeper chocolate flavor, replace chocolate chips with 2 tbsp cacao powder, add maple syrup to taste, and a tsp of cold coffee. Find current links to the ingredients and equipment I used, and nutritional studies at: greensmoothiegourmet.com/resources/

Ginger Cayenne Detox Shot

Cure the three o'clock slump with this bright shot, a golden immunity-booster. Ginger is a go-to remedy for ailments ranging in seriousness from colds to hypertension. Combined with lemon, the pair is credit for clearing mysterious issues to skin, joints, digestion. Cayenne pepper fires up a metabolism-boosting detox, while coconut water provides essential minerals and cell-boosting potassium.

MAKES 2 (2-OUNCE) SHOTS

1/2 cup coconut water

2 tbsp lemon juice

2 inches ginger

1/2 tsp cayenne pepper

NOURISHING
HYDRATING DRINKS

Immunity & Detox

PREPARATION

1. Refrigerate the coconut water overnight.
2. Peel the fresh ginger knob. Leaving some skin specs are fine since you will be filtering out the pulp. Chop the peeled garlic into small chunks. Crush the chunks with a garlic press, and capture the resulting juice and pulp in a bowl.
3. Microwave a lemon at 10 seconds to allow optimum release of lemon juice. Juice the lemon and store juice you don't use in the refrigerator.
4. Add the coconut water, ginger juice and pulp, lemon juice and cayenne pepper to a high-speed blender or food processor for a rougher blend.
5. Blend for about 2 minutes at high speed. Pour the mixture through a fine-mesh strainer into a measuring cup. Retain the pulp for 24 hours refrigerated to add to smoothies.
6. Divide the resulting juice into small portions, typically around 1-2 ounces each. Refrigerate and have one a day, either in the morning or to boost you out of an afternoon slump.

protein 1.1 fiber 1.5 fat 0.6 calories 35 sugars 2.1 carbs 6.6

SWAPS, BOOSTS & SOURCES

Tools useful for this recipe include a fine-mesh strainer, a garlic press, and 2-ounce glass shot glasses with screw tops for storage. Find current links to the ingredients and equipment I used, and nutritional studies at: greensmoothiegourmet.com/resources/

200 ml
100 ml

Iced Blue Spirulina Latte

Spirulina powder is a popular superfood that is extraordinarily high in nutrients, including B vitamins, iron, zinc and more essentials hard to get through eating. Spirulina is an algae and can come in green, or a popular blue version that I used here for my latte. And it is so respected for its antioxidant and anti-stress properties that NASA is studying it to be grown in space for the nourishment of astronauts.

MAKES 2 LATTES

1 cup oat milk (or your favorite)
1/2 tsp blue spirulina (Blue Majik)
1/4 cup coconut water
1/2 tbsp cinnamon

NOURISHING
HYDRATING DRINKS

Good Mood Food
& Stress-Reducer

PREPARATION

1. Stir together the milk and cinnamon.
2. Dissolve the spirulina powder in a small bowl with a few tablespoons of warm water, until you have a blue paste. Add the coconut water so you have about 2/3 cup of blue water.
3. Pour this into another 1/2 cup of water and ice cubes, and swirl to combine.
4. Pour the milk over the blue spirulina and enjoy!

protein 10.4 fiber 3.3 fat 3 calories 170 sugars 20.6 carbs 29.6

SWAPS, BOOSTS & SOURCES

Swap the coconut water or oat milk for hemp milk (find unrefrigerated in boxed milk section) for a denser drink with healthy fats. This recipe is not sweet; add maple syrup to taste if needed. Find current links to the ingredients and equipment I used, and nutritional studies at: greensmoothiegourmet.com/resources/

Cherry Rose Moon Milk

The perfect sleep-inducing drink should have a few essentials the body needs to be lulled into sleep, including melatonin, vitamin D, magnesium and potassium. Foods like cherries and oats are prime candidates for this role, and they happen to create a delicious sleepy-time beverage. Add in coconut oil for a touch of filling, healthy fats, and a delicate soothing rose scent. Good night.

MAKES 2 CUPS

2 cups oat milk (plus more to froth)
1 cup cherries, fresh or frozen
1 tbsp coconut oil
2 tsp rose water

NOURISHING
HYDRATING DRINKS

Sleep Support

PREPARATION

1. Pit and pulverize the cherries in a bowl with the back of spoon.
2. Add the cherries, milk, and coconut oil into a pot and simmer for a few minutes, stirring constantly. I usually shut off the heat as the liquid steams, just prior to boil.
3. Let the pot cool, then pour through a strainer into two mugs. Hold back some milk to make froth. Refrigerate the cherry pulp to add to the next day's smoothie.
4. Stir a tsp of rose water into each mug.
5. Froth up milk with a hand-frother. Top the mugs, and sprinkle with cinnamon.

protein 2.8 fiber 2.3 fat 8.3 calories 162 sugars 16 carbs 21.5

SWAPS, BOOSTS & SOURCES

The cherries are the source of melatonin, but if you don't have them, the remaining ingredients will still support sleep. You can also add crushed walnuts, also high in melatonin, or pumpkin seeds, high in magnesium. Find current links to the ingredients and equipment I used, and nutritional studies at: greensmoothiegourmet.com/resources/

Watermelon Kiwi Blender Juice

Drinking this as a juice, not a smoothie, speeds up nutrient absorption, resulting in a quick burst of energy. And it helps that a good portion of this recipe is watermelon. Low in calories, high in vital nutrients, and being 90% water, the melon keeps you hydrated and feeling full. Fresh mint stimulates digestive enzymes, speeding up energy production. Kiwi boosts metabolism, while leafy greens, being high in iron, hike energy stores.

MAKES 2 CUPS

1 cup watermelon
1/2 cup fresh mint
1 cup kiwi
1/2 cup fresh spinach

PREPARATION

1. The night before, cut the watermelon and kiwi into chunks and freeze.
2. The day of juice-making, remove the fruit chunks from the freezer and set them in the high-speed blender jar about 10 minutes before blending to thaw them a bit while still keeping them frosty.
3. Wash mint and leafy greens, chop them roughly and add them to the blender.
4. Blend for about 2 minutes at high speed. Pour the mixture through a fine-mesh strainer into a measuring cup. Retain the pulp for 24 hours refrigerated to add to smoothies.
5. Divide the resulting juice into two cups.

protein 2.4 fiber 4.7 fat 0.8 calories 89 sugars 12.7 carbs 20.9

SWAPS, BOOSTS & SOURCES

Swap the spinach for arugula or kale, but both have a stronger green flavor. Find current links to the ingredients and equipment I used, and nutritional studies at: greensmoothiegourmet.com/resources/

Butterfly Pea Collagen Cooler

Here I go with more blue drinks. Very a la Star Wars, I know. But seriously blue drinks got game! This one is made from a powder from a butterfly pea plant, a flower from Southeast Asia. The tea is rich in age-defying antioxidants, and high in anthocyanins, compounds that build and restore skin collagen. Supplement the drink with plant-based collagen.

MAKES 2 SERVINGS

2 butterfly pea flower tea bags
2 cups ice cubes
1/2 cup hemp milk (or almond)
2 collagen capsules

NOURISHING
HYDRATING DRINKS

Hair, Skin &
Nail Support

PREPARATION

1. Steep the butterfly pea flower tea in 1 cup of hot water for 10 minutes for deepest color. Then set it in the refrigerator to cool, about 10 minutes.
2. Break open or crush your collagen capsules and stir into the milk. Choose a thick milk, such as hemp, oat or your favorite creamer. I did not add sweetener but if you like sweet tea, add 1 tsp of maple syrup into the milk and taste-test.
3. Put the ice cubes in two serving glasses. Pour the tea over the ice.
4. Pour the creamer over the tea in both glasses. The thicker your chosen milk, the more dramatic the swirl effect will be.
5. Drink immediately.

protein 0.5 fiber 0 fat 2 calories 137 sugars 0 carbs 0.3

SWAPS, BOOSTS & SOURCES

If you are not ready to try butterfly pea tea, make the same drink with beet powder. It will be a vibrant pink. Find current links to the ingredients and equipment I used, and nutritional studies at: greensmoothiegourmet.com/resources/

Macchiato Overnight Buckwheat

A Macchiato, the well-known coffee drink, is a caffeinated drink served with a dash of frothy steamed milk. Here, it takes a healthy turn, and is actually a meal-replacer with the nutritious and filling buckwheat groats. Date paste serves as a healthier, iron-rich sweetener, and adds a bit of caramel flavor to further authenticate this popular drink. If buckwheat groats are new to you, find them in your grocery store bulk food area.

MAKES ONE SERVING

1/2 cup buckwheat groats (rinsed, soaked)
1 cup coffee (with milk)
1/2 cup date paste (6 dates + 3 tbsp of water)
1 tbsp cinnamon

PREPARATION

1. To prep for this recipe, put the buckwheat groats and dates in separate containers of water in the refrigerator overnight to soften them. The next day, rinse them both, pit the dates and you are ready to make your macchiato.
2. Make the date paste first. You only need two tablespoons of date paste for this coffee, but it is easier to blend at least 1/2 cup. Store the remaining date paste in the refrigerator and use it as a healthier sweetener.
3. Make coffee the way you normally drink it, although if you normally drink it black, I suggest you add milk today to make this macchiato.
4. Into one cup of coffee, stir in the soaked but drained groats, cinnamon.
5. Pour the mixture in a serving jar, and top with 2 tablespoons of date paste, and foamed milk with a dusting of cinnamon.
6. Eat right away.

protein 3.5 fiber 3.6 fat 0.6 calories 126 sugars 11.3 carbs 29.2

SWAPS, BOOSTS & SOURCES

Reduce date paste to make it less sweet. Buckwheat groats are incredibly nutritious, gluten-free, wheat-free and nut-free. Find them in with bulk foods or online. Sometimes called kasha. Find current links to the ingredients and equipment I used, and nutritional studies at: greensmoothiegourmet.com/resources/

A Healthy Capsule Pantry

A *capsule pantry* is an intentionally streamlined list of healthy ingredients that can be combined to produce many different recipes. The idea is a spin off the familiar fashion industry concept of a *capsule wardrobe*, or a selection of a few essential items that can work together in multiple ways to produce many different outfits. Here I share my *capsule pantry* full of ingredients used to make the recipes in this book, and more.

PRODUCE

apples
asparagus
avocado
bananas
beets
berries
carrots
cauliflower
citrus
cucumbers
dates
garlic
ginger
herbs
kiwi
onions
leafy greens
melon
potatoes
tomatoes
watermelon
zucchini

FRIDGE/FREEZER

nut & oat milk (almond, cashew, oat)
yogurt (cashew, coconut)
coconut milk (full-fat)
coconut cream
coconut milk (lite)
vegan butter
frozen fruits (blueberries, cherries, mango, pineapple)
vegetable broth
ketchup (free of sugar)
apple cider vinegar
lemon juice

NUTS & SEEDS

(raw, unsalted)
cashews, almonds, walnuts, pecans, macadamia nuts, sunflower seeds, pumpkin seeds, chia seeds, ground flax seeds, hemp seeds, sesame seeds

NUT & SEED BUTTERS

(homemade or bought)
cashew butter
almond butter

sunflower seed butter
tahini (sesame seed butter)
coconut butter (made from shredded coconut)

DRY FOODS

quinoa
buckwheat groats
gluten-free rolled oats
coconut (shredded)
coffee
lentil pasta
chickpea pasta
ramen noodles
dried fruits
pozole
lentils (dry)

CANNED FOOD

white beans (canned, navy)
chickpeas (canned)
pumpkin puree
sweet potato puree
butternut squash puree

FLOURS

almond meal, fine almond flour, coconut flour, chickpea flour, oat flour, self-rising flour, gluten-free all-purpose flour, 1-to-1 baking flour

CHOCOLATE

dark chocolate bar (70%-85% cacao)
dark chocolate chips (dairy-free)
cacao butter (blond)
cacao nibs
cacao powder

SPICES

cinnamon, Italian spices, pumpkin pie spices, turmeric, cumin, garlic powder, onion powder, ginger, red pepper flakes, cloves, cayenne, nutritional yeast

SUPERFOODS

acai powder, goji berries, pink pitaya (frozen), blue spirulina, matcha powder, tocos powder, butterfly pea tea

BAKING NEEDS

vanilla paste, baking soda, baking powder, organic cane sugar, coconut palm sugar, organic powdered sugar

OILS

olive oil, coconut oil (virgin), coconut oil (refined)

SWEETENERS

fresh Medjool dates
organic maple syrup

EXTRAS

olives (canned) , artichoke hearts (canned)
diced green chilis, probiotics, rose water, quality tomato sauce

ESSENTIAL EQUIPMENT

blender (preferably high-speed)
food processor (7-cup)
pyrex measuring (2) cup, mixing bowls, measuring spoons and cups, pans, parchment

Index

D

F

G

K

L

M

T

Made in the USA
Middletown, DE
22 November 2020